MW01062352

THE JADE MOUNTAIN

THE JADE MOUNTAIN

A CHINESE ANTHOLOGY

Being Three Hundred Poems of the T'ang Dynasty 618-906

Translated

by

WITTER BYNNER

from the texts of

KIANG KANG-HU

VINTAGE BOOKS

A Division of Random House
New York

Library of Congress Cataloging in Publication Data

Sun, Chu, 1711-1778, comp.
    The jade mountain.

    1. Chinese poetry—Translations into English.
2. English poetry—Translations from Chinese.
I. Bynner, Witter, 1881-1968, tr. II. Kiang, Kang-hu,
1883-   III. Title. IV. Title: Three hundred poems
of the T'ang dynasty.
PL2658.E3S8 1972   895.1'1'308   72-1396
ISBN 0-394-71841-0

Manufactured in the United States of America

Vintage Books Edition, September 1972

WE JOIN
IN DEDICATING OUR TRANSLATIONS
TO
ALBERT M. BENDER

"Literature endures like the universal spirit,
And its breath becomes a part of the vitals of all men."

LI SHANG-YIN

CONTENTS

Introduction

I

POETRY AND CULTURE

by Witter Bynner

LIKE MOST of us who have been schooled in this western world, I was afforded in my youth a study of culture flowing mainly from two sources, the Greek and the Hebrew. I had come to feel that poetic literature must contain streams from one or the other of these two sources: on the one hand the clean, objective, symmetrical, athletic beauty of the Greek; on the other hand the turgid, subjective, distorted, elaborated beauty of the Hebrew. Like my fellow students, I had been offered nothing of the literatures of the Far East. I am still doubtful that I could ever feel any real adherence to the ornate and entranced literature of India; but I have come by accident into as close touch with Chinese poetry as a westerner is able to come without a knowledge of the Chinese tongue. And I feel with conviction that in the matter of poetry I have begun to receive a new, finer, and deeper education than ever came to me from the Hebrew or the Greek.

Centuries ago cultivated Chinese had reached the intellectual saturation which has tired the mind of the modern European. The Chinese gentleman knew the ancient folk-songs, compiled by Confucius. He knew also, all around him, a profoundly rich civilization, a more poised and particularized sophistication than we

westerners have yet attained. Through the Asian centuries every-
one has written verse. In fact, from early imperial days down to
these even worse disordered days of the Republic, the sense of
poetry as a natural and solacing part of life has lasted among the
Chinese people. Whether or not the individual may form or enjoy
his poetry in metrical shape, he is constantly aware of the kinship
between the beauty of the world and the beauty of imaginative
phrase. On any Chinese mountain-climb toward a temple, rock
after rock with its terse and suggestive inscription will bear witness
to this temper. So will the street cries of the peddlers, or the names
of the tea-houses, and on many hill-tops and lake-sides the casual
but reverent jottings of this or that anonymous appreciator of
natural beauty. When Whitman said: " To have great poets there
must be great audiences too," he must have had in the back of
his mind enriched generations like the Elizabethan in England
or like almost any generation in China. In those great audiences
each man, to the limit of his capacity and with natural ease, was
a poet.

There is a simple secret in these generations. It is told in a
pamphlet by a venerable Chinese scholar who, until his death two
years ago, was still with infinite passion adhering to the precepts
of his ancestors, and with infinite patience, acceptably expressed
by the way among foreigners, adhering to his conviction that
foreigners impair the health of China. His name is Ku Hung-
ming. His pamphlet, written in English, one of the five languages
which he could use, is called *The Spirit of the Chinese People*.
In it he advances, as reason for the eternal youth of the Chinese
people, the fact that the average Chinese has managed to maintain
within himself the head of a man and the heart of a child. On this

brief he is absorbingly interesting, explaining the continuance of Chinese culture, the only ancient culture still racially existent. My immediate concern with his brief is more special. I detect in it something that he does not specify: a reason for the continuance of poetry as a live factor among his people and, more than that, the best reason I know of for the persistence of poetry anywhere among cultured races.

Music may be the most intimate of the arts, I am not sure. Except for simple melodies, music is beyond the reach of any individual who is not a technician. Painting and sculpture are obviously arts expressing themselves in single given objects, which, although they may be copied and so circulated, are for the most part accessible only to the privileged or to those who make pilgrimages. Poetry more than any other of the arts may be carried about by a man either in his own remembering heart or else in compact and easily available printed form. It belongs to anyone. It is of all the arts the closest to a man; and it will so continue to be, in spite of the apparent shocks given it by the noises of modern commerce and science and jazz.

It has been a common occurrence in China that poets, even the best of them, devote their earlier years to some form of public service. Century after century, Chinese poems reflect this deep devotion of their authors to the good of the State — their unwavering allegiance to righteousness, even when it meant demotion or exile or death. In modern western times there have been periods when poetry has seemed to be a candle-lit and thin-blooded occupation. I venture to surmise that poetry written in that sort of atmosphere grows with time less and less valid, less and less noticed. As a matter of fact, the outstanding English poets have been acutely concerned with the happiness of their fellow men and have given themselves warmly to public causes in which they believed. Similarly, present-day poets in America, with amazingly few exceptions, have clustered to the defence of noble souls at bay like Eugene Debs, or have been quick to protest against doubtful justice, as in the case of Sacco and Vanzetti. This sort of zeal may not result in poetry of a high order immediately connected with the specific cause; but there is no question that but for this bravery, this heat on behalf of man's better nature, there would not be in the hearts of the poets so fine a crucible for their more personal alchemies.

Let me say a more general word than Dr. Kiang's as to the characteristic method of the best Chinese poetry. I am not referring to the technical means by which a Chinese poet makes his words balanced and melodious. The discovery which has largely undone my previous convictions as to the way of writing poetry has rather to do with use of substance than with turns of expression. Mencius said long ago, in reference to the Odes collected by Confucius: "Those who explain the Odes must not insist on one term so as to do violence to a sentence, nor on a sentence so as to do violence to the general scope. They must try with their thoughts to meet that scope, and then they will apprehend it." In the poetry of the west we are accustomed to let our appreciative minds accept with joy this or that passage in a poem — to prefer the occasional glitter of a jewel to the straight light of the sun. The Chinese poet seldom lets any portion of what he is saying unbalance the entirety. Moreover, with the exception of a particular class of writing — adulatory verse written for the court — Chinese poetry rarely trespasses beyond the bounds of actuality. Whereas western poets will take actualities as points of departure for exaggeration or fantasy, or else as shadows of contrast against dreams of unreality, the great Chinese poets accept the world exactly as they find it in all its terms, and with profound simplicity find therein sufficient solace. Even in phraseology they seldom talk about one thing in terms of another, but are able enough and sure enough as artists to make the ultimately exact terms become the beautiful terms. If a metaphor is used, it is a metaphor directly relating to the theme, not something borrowed from the ends of the earth. The metaphor must be concurrent with the action or flow of the poem; not merely superinduced, but an integral part of both the scene and the emotion.

Wordsworth, of our poets, comes closest to the Chinese; but their poetry cleaves even nearer to nature than his. They perform the miracle of identifying the wonder of beauty with common sense. Rather, they prove that the simplest common sense, the most salutary, and the most nearly universal, is the sense of the beauty of nature, quickened and yet sobered by the wistful warmth of human friendship.

For our taste, used as we are to the operatic in poetry, the substance of Chinese poems seems often mild or even trivial; but if we will be honest with ourselves and with our appreciation of what is lastingly important, we shall find these very same poems to be momentous details in the immense patience of beauty. They are the heart of an intimate letter. They bring the true, the beautiful, the everlasting, into simple, easy touch with the human, the homely, and the immediate. And I predict that future western poets will go to school with the masters of the T'ang Dynasty, as well as with the masters of the golden age of Greece, or with the

Hebrew prophets, or with the English dramatists or romanticists — to learn how best may be expressed, for themselves and others, that passionate patience which is the core of life.

It is not necessary that culture bring about the death of poetry, as it did in the Rome of Virgil. The cynics are wrong who see in our future no place for an art which belongs, they say, to the childhood of the race. The head of a man and the heart of a child working together as in the Chinese have made possible with one race and may make possible with any race, even in the thick of the most intricate culture, the continuance of the purest poetry.

Because of the absence of tenses, of personal pronouns and of connectives generally, the translator of Chinese poetry, like the Chinese reader himself, has considerable leeway as to interpretation. If even in English, so much more definite a language, there may be varying interpretations of a given poem, it is no wonder that critics and annotators have differed as to the meaning of poems in Chinese. There have been frequent instances in this volume where Dr. Kiang and I have discussed several possible meanings of a poem and have chosen for translation into the more definite language the meaning we preferred.

With his sanction I have decided that for readers in English it is better to eliminate or use only seldom the names of places and persons not highly important to the sense of a poem: to use "southern" or "eastern," for instance, instead of regional names unfamiliar in the Occident; to indicate the person meant when the poem, according to Chinese custom, employs the name and attributes of some other similar well-known person, and to embody in the English text something of the significance which would be conveyed to any Chinese reader, but not to western readers, by historical or literary allusions.

At the risk of criticism, I have made certain reasonable compromises. I have used the sometimes inaccurate term " Tartar " instead of " Hun " or " barbarian," the term " China " instead of " Han," the term " Turkestan " when it roughly corresponded to the ancient term. There are many other approximations which have seemed advisable. Once in a while, for good reason, I have changed a title. And there are occasional unimportant omissions. I have omitted, for instance, the " ninth-born " or " eleventh-born," frequently added in the original to names of persons, and meaning the ninth or eleventh child in a family. Whenever possible, I have avoided phraseology which, natural and familiar in Chinese, would be exotic or quaint in English; I have hoped rather to accent in these T'ang masterpieces the human and universal qualities by which they have endured.

WITTER BYNNER

Santa Fé, New Mexico

II

CHINESE POETRY

by Kiang Kang-hu

Poems of the Early Period

CHINESE POETRY began with our written history about 5500 years ago. The oldest poems now extant were written by the Emperor Yao (2357 B.C.); and one of them was adopted as the Chinese national song in the beginning of the Republic, because Yao was in reality a life president of the most ancient republic in the world, and this poem expresses the republican spirit. Shun and Yü, the other two sagacious presidents, left with us also some poems. Their works, together with other verses by following emperors and statesmen, may be found in our classics and official histories.

In the Chou Dynasty (1122–256 B.C.) poetry became more important, not only to individual and social life, but also to the government. Emperors used to travel over all the feudal states and to collect the most popular and typical poems or songs. The collection being then examined by the official historians and musicians, public opinion and the welfare of the people in the respective states would thus be ascertained and attested. In the ceremonies of sacrifice, inter-state convention, official banquet, and school and military exercises, various poems were sung and harmonized with music. Poetry in this period was not a special literary task for scholars, but a means of expression common to both sexes of all classes.

The Classical Poems

One of the five Confucian classics is the *Book of Poetry*. It is a selection of poems of the Chou Dynasty, classified under different types. This selection was made by Confucius out of the governmental collections of many states. It contains three hundred and eleven poems, all of high standard, both as literature and as music. Since the loss of the Confucian *Book of Music* during the period of the Great Destruction (221–211 B.C.) the musical significance of this classic can hardly be traced, but its literary value remains and the distinction of the classical poems, which can never be duplicated.

Poems Since the Han Dynasty

The classical poems were usually composed of lines of four characters, or words, with every other line rhymed. Lines were allowed, however, of more or fewer words. Under the reign of the Emperor Wu (140–87 B.C.) of the Western Han Dynasty new types of poetry were introduced; and the five-character and seven-character poems became popular and have dominated ever since. The Emperor himself invented the latter; while Li Ling and Su Wu, two of his statesmen-generals, wrote their verses in the former type. The number of characters of each line was uniform; no irregular line might occur. These two types were afterwards named the "ancient" or "unruled" poems. Nearly all poems before the T'ang Dynasty were in this form. The Emperor Wu introduced also the Po Liang style, which is a seven-character poem with every line rhyming in the last word. Po Liang was the name of a pavilion in the Emperor's garden where, while he banqueted his literary attendants, each wrote one line to complete a long poem. This has been a favourite game among Chinese poets.

The Poems of the T'ang Dynasty

As many a dynasty in Chinese history is marked by some phase of success representing the thought and life of that period, the T'ang Dynasty is commonly recognized as the golden age of poetry. Beginning with the founder of the dynasty, down to the last ruler, almost every one of the emperors was a great lover and patron of poetry, and many were poets themselves. A special tribute should be paid to the Empress Wu Chao or the "Woman Emperor" (684–704), through whose influence poetry became a requisite in examinations for degrees and an important course leading to official promotion. This made every official as well as every scholar a poet. The poems required in the examination, after long years of gradual development, followed a formula, and many regulations were established. Not only must the length of a line be limited to a certain number of characters, usually five or seven, but also the length of a poem was limited to a certain number of lines, usually four or eight or twelve. The maintenance of rhymes, the parallelism of characters, and the balance of tones were other rules considered essential. This is called the "modern" or "ruled" poetry. In the Ch'ing or Manchu Dynasty the examination poem was standardized as a five-character-line poem of sixteen lines with every other line rhymed. This "eight-rhyme" poem was accompanied by the famous "eight-legged" literature (a form of literature divided into eight sections) as a guiding light for entrance into mandarin life.

The above-mentioned rules of poetry applied first only to examination poems. But afterwards they became a common exercise with "modern" or "ruled" poems in general. Chinese poetry since the T'ang Dynasty has followed practically only two forms, the "modern" or "ruled" form and the "ancient" or "unruled" form. A poet usually writes both. The "eight-rhyme" poem, however, was practised for official examinations only.

The progress of T'ang poetry may be viewed through a division into four periods, as distinguished by different styles and a differing spirit. There were, of course, exceptional works, especially at the transient points, and it is difficult to draw an exact boundary-line between any two periods. The first period is approximately from A.D. 620 to 700, the second from 700 to 780, the third from 780 to 850, and the fourth from 850 to 900. The second period, corresponding to the summer season of the year, is regarded as the most celebrated epoch. Its representative figures are Li Po (705–762), the genie of poetry; Tu Fu, (712–720), the sage of poetry; Wang Wêi (699–759) and Mêng Hao-jan (689–740), the two hermit-poets, and Ts'ên Ts'an (given degree, 744) and Wêi Ying-wu (about 740–830), the two magistrate-poets. The first period is represented by Chang Yüeh (667–730) and Chang Chiu-ling (673–740), two premiers, and by Sung Chih-wên (died 710) and Tu Shên-yen (between the seventh and the eighth centuries); the third, by Yuan Chên (779–832) and Po Chü-yi (772–846), two cabinet ministers, and by Han Yü (768–824) and Liu Tsung-yüan (773–819), two master *literati* more famous for their prose writing than for their verse; and the fourth, by Wên T'ing-yün (ninth century) and Li Shang-yin (813–858), the founders of the Hsi K'un school, and by Hsü Hun (given degree, 832) and Yao Hê (A.D. 9th century). All these poets had their works published in a considerable number of volumes. Secondary poets in the T'ang Dynasty were legion.

Poems after the T'ang Dynasty

Since the T'ang Dynasty, poetry has become even more popular. Its requirement as one of the subjects in the governmental examinations has continued, for a thousand years, to the end of the last century, through all changes of dynasty. Many great poets have arisen during this time. Su Shih (1036–1101), Huang T'ing-chien (1050–1110), Ou-yang Hsiu (1007–1072) and Lu Yu (1125–1209), of the Sung Dynasty, are names as celebrated as those great names of the second period of the T'ang Dynasty. But people still honour the works of the T'ang poets as the model for ever-coming generations, though many of more varied literary taste prefer the Sung works.

Chao Mêng-fu (1254–1322) of the Yüan Dynasty and Yüan Hao-wên (1190–1258) of the Kin Dynasty were the shining stars of that dark age. Many poets of the Ming Dynasty, such as Liu Chi (1311–1375), Sung Lien (1310–1381), Li Tung-yang (1447–1516), and Ho Ching-ming (1483–1521) were very famous. Still greater poets lived in the Ch'ing Dynasty. Ch'ien Ch'ien-yi (1581–1664), Wu Wêi-yeh (1609–1671), Wang Shih-chêng (1526–1593), Chao Yi (1727–1814), Chiang Shih-ch'üan (1725–1784), Yuan Mêi (1715–1797), Huang Ching-jên (1749–1783), and Chang Wên-t'ao (1764–1814) are some of the immortals. Their works are by no means inferior to those in the previous dynasties.

Literature differs from science. It changes according to times and conditions, but shows, on the whole, neither rapid improvement nor gradual betterment. Later writings might appear to be more expressive and therefore more inspiring, but the dignity and beauty of ancient works are inextinguishable and even unapproached. This is especially true of poetry and of the T'ang poems, for the reason that during those three hundred years the thinking capacity and the working energy of all excellent citizens in the Empire were encouraged and induced to this single subject. Neither before nor after has there been such an age for poetry.

Selections of the T'ang Poems

Hundreds of collections and selections of T'ang poems have been published during the succeeding dynasties. Two compiled in the Ch'ing Dynasty are considered the best. One is the *Complete Collection of T'ang Poems* and the other is the *Three Hundred T'ang Poems*. These two have no similarity in nature and in purpose. The first is an imperial edition aiming to include every line of existing T'ang poetry: which amounts to 48,900 poems by 2,200 poets in 900 volumes. The second is but a small text-book for elementary students, giving only 311 better-known works by 77 of the better-known writers, the same number of poems as in the Confucian Classic of Poetry. This selection was made by an anonymous editor who signed himself " Hêng T'ang T'uêi Shih " or " A Retired Scholar at the Lotus Pool," first published in the reign of the Emperor Ch'ien Lung (1735–1795). The title of this selection was based upon a common saying: " By reading thoroughly three hundred T'ang poems, one will write verse without learning."

In the preface the compiler assures us that "this is but a family reader for children; but it will hold good until our hair is white." This statement, as years have passed, has proved true. The collection has always stood in China as the most popular volume of poetry, for poets and for the mass of the people alike. Even illiterates are familiar with the title of the book and with lines from it. Other selections may be of a higher standard and please scholars better, but none can compare with this in extensive circulation and accessible influence.

The anthology in Chinese is in two volumes. The first contains all "ancient" or "unruled" poems, and the second all "modern" or "ruled" poems. The former is again divided into two parts of five-character lines and seven-character lines, the latter into four parts: (1) eight five-character lines, (2) eight seven-character lines, (3) four five-character lines, and (4) four seven-character lines. In learning Chinese poems the order is always reversed. The shorter line of fewer characters should come first. We have, however, rearranged the volume in English, according to poets rather than to poetic technique, the poets following one another in the alphabetical order of their surnames. (The surname in Chinese comes first.) Under each poet we have kept the following order of poems:

1. Modern poems of four five-character lines.
2. Modern poems of four seven-character lines.
3. Modern poems of eight five-character lines.
4. Modern poems of eight seven-character lines.
5. Ancient poems of five-character lines.
6. Ancient poems of seven-character lines.

Various Poetic Regulations and Forms

There are more strict regulations in writing poems in Chinese than in any other language. This is because Chinese is the only living language governed by the following rules: First, it is made of individual hierographic characters; second, each character or word is monosyllabic; and third, each character has its fixed tone. Hence certain very important regulations in Chinese poetry are little considered or even unknown to the poetry of other languages. For instance, the avoidance of using a word twice, the parallelism of words of the same nature and the balancing of words of different tones, all need special preliminary explanation.

The first of these regulations is possible only in Chinese poetry. We find many long poems with hundreds or even thousands of characters, and not a single one repeated, as in the form of *p'ai-lü* or "arranged rule." The second means that all the characters of one line should parallel as parts of speech those of the next line; thus noun with noun, adjective with adjective, verb with verb, etc. Even in the same parts of speech, nouns designating animals should be parallel, adjectives of colour, numbers, etc. The third means that all the characters of a line should balance, in the opposite group of tones, those of the next line. There are five tones in the Chinese written language. The first is called the upper even tone; the second, the lower even tone; the third, the upper tone; the fourth, the departing tone; and the fifth, the entering tone. The first two are in one group, named "even tones," and the last three are in the other group and named "uneven tones." Thus, if any character in a line is of the even group, the character which balances with it in the next line should be of the uneven group, and vice versa.

These strict regulations, though very important to "modern" or "ruled" poems, do not apply to "ancient" or "unruled" poems. The ancient form is very liberal. There are but two regulations for it — namely, a limit to the number of characters in each line, five or seven; and rhyme on the last character of every other line. The seven-character "ancient" poem gives even more leeway. It may have irregular lines of more or fewer characters, and every line may rhyme as in the Po Liang style.

There are also, as in English, perfect rhymes and allowable rhymes. The perfect rhymes are standardized by an Imperial Rhyming Dictionary. In this dictionary all characters are arranged, first according to the five tones, and then to different rhymes. The two even tones have 30 rhymes; the third, 29; the fourth, 30; and the fifth, a very short sound, only 17. These rhymes are so grouped, following the old classical pronunciation, that some rhyming words may seem to the modern ear discordant. The allowable rhymes include words that rhymed before the standard was made. The "modern" poem must observe perfect rhymes; the "ancient" poem is permitted allowable rhymes. Again, the former should use only one rhyme of the even tones; the latter may use many different rhymes of different tones in one poem.

The "modern" poem has also its fixed pattern of tones. There are four patterns for the five-character poems and four for the seven-character poems. The signs used in the following charts are commonly adopted in Chinese poetry: — indicates an even tone; | indicates an uneven tone; ⊤ indicates that the character should be of an even tone, but that an uneven is permitted; ⊥ indicates the reverse; ⊖ indicates the rhyme.

TONE PATTERNS FOR FIVE-CHARACTER MODERN POEMS

A

```
8  7  6  5  4  3  2  1
⊥  T  T  ⊥  ⊥  T  T  ⊥
|  —  —  |  |  —  —  |
|  —  |  —  |  —  |  —
—  |  |  —  —  |  |  —
⊖  |  ⊖  |  ⊖  |  ⊖  |
```

B

```
8  7  6  5  4  3  2  1
T  ⊥  ⊥  T  T  ⊥  ⊥  T
—  |  |  —  —  |  |  —
|  —  |  —  |  —  |  —
|  —  —  |  |  —  —  |
⊖  |  ⊖  |  ⊖  |  ⊖  |
```

C

```
8  7  6  5  4  3  2  1
⊥  T  T  ⊥  ⊥  T  T  ⊥
|  —  —  |  |  —  —  |
|  —  |  —  |  —  |  |
—  |  |  —  —  |  |  |
⊖  |  ⊖  |  ⊖  |  ⊖  ⊖
```

D

```
8  7  6  5  4  3  2  1
T  ⊥  ⊥  T  T  ⊥  ⊥  T
—  |  |  —  —  |  |  —
|  —  |  —  |  —  |  |
|  —  —  |  |  —  —  |
⊖  |  ⊖  |  ⊖  i  ⊖  ⊖
```

First line ⎫
Second line ⎭ First pair ⎫
Third line ⎫   ⎬ First group
Fourth line ⎭ Second pair ⎭

Fifth line   ⎫
Sixth line   ⎭ Third pair ⎫
Seventh line ⎫   ⎬ Second group
Eighth line ⎭ Fourth pair ⎭

TONE PATTERNS FOR SEVEN-CHARACTER MODERN POEMS

A

```
8 7 6 5 4 3 2 1
⊥ T T ⊥ ⊥ T T ⊥
| - - | | - - |
T ⊥ ⊥ T T ⊥ ⊥ T
- | | - - | | -
| - | - | - | -
| - - | | - - |
⊖ | ⊖ | ⊖ | ⊖ |
```

B

```
8 7 6 5 4 3 2 1
T ⊥ ⊥ T T ⊥ ⊥ T
- | | - - | | -
⊥ T T ⊥ ⊥ T T ⊥
| - - | | - - |
| - | - | - | -
- | | - - | | -
⊖ | ⊖ | ⊖ | ⊖ |
```

C

```
8 7 6 5 4 3 2 1
⊥ T T ⊥ ⊥ T T ⊥
| - - | | - - |
T ⊥ ⊥ T T ⊥ ⊥ T
- | | - - | | -
| - | - | - | |
| - - | | - - |
⊖ | ⊖ | ⊖ | ⊖ ⊖
```

D

```
8 7 6 5 4 3 2 1
T ⊥ ⊥ T T ⊥ ⊥ T
- | | - - | | -
⊥ T T ⊥ ⊥ T T ⊥
| - - | | - - |
| - | - | - | |
- | | - - | | -
⊖ | ⊖ | ⊖ | ⊖ ⊖
```

For further and clearer explanation I use as an example the following poem:

Sur-name	杜	Tu⁴	Cabinet	閣	Kê⁵
given name (Author)	甫	Fu³	night (Title)	夜	yeh⁴

Heaven's	天	T'ien¹	year late (the)	歲 暮	Suêi⁴ mu⁴
limit	涯	ya²	negative force	陰	yin¹
frost (and)	霜	shuang¹	(and) positive force	陽	yang²
snow	雪	hsüeh⁵	urge	催	ts'uêi¹
brighten	霽	chi⁴	(the) short	短	tuan³
(the) cold	寒	han²	day-light.	景	ching²
night.	宵	hsiao¹			

(Upon the) three	三	San¹	(At the) fifth	五	wu³
mountains (the)	峽	hsia⁵	watch (the)	更	kêng¹
stars (and)	星	hsing¹	drum (and)	鼓	ku³

English			English		
milk-way's	河	he²	bugle's	角	chüeh⁵
shadows	影	ying³	sound	聲	shêng¹
move	動	tung⁴	sad	悲	pêi¹
(and)	搖	yao²	(and)	壯	chuang⁴
wave.			brave.		

English			English		
Barbarian	夷	i²	Wild	野	yeh⁸
songs	歌	kê¹	sobs	哭	k'u⁵
every	是	shih⁴	(of)	幾	chi⁸
place	處	ch'u⁴	many	家	chia¹
arise	起	ch'i³	homes	聞	wên²
(from)			(are)		
fishers	漁	yü²	heard		
(and)			(in)		
wood-cutters.	樵	ch'iao²	fighting	戰	chan⁴
			(and)	伐	fa⁵
			attacking.		

English			English		
Human	人	Jên²	(The)	臥	Wo⁴
affairs	事	shih⁴	Lying		
(in)			Dragon	龍	lung²
messages	音	yin¹	(and)		
(and)			(the)	躍	yüeh⁵
letters	書	shu¹	Jumping		
(may)			Horse	馬	ma³
let it be	漫	man⁴	finally		
silent			(became)	終	chung¹
(and)	寂	chi⁵	yellow	黃	huang²
solitude.	寥	liao²	dusts.	土	t'u³

The first group of a "ruled poem" is named the "rising pair"; the second, the "receiving pair"; the third, the "turning pair"; and the fourth, the "concluding pair."

This example shows us that in writing a "modern" or "ruled" poem many essential regulations are involved. They may be summed up in six rules:

1. Limitation of lines (four or eight, though the *p'ai lü* or "arranged rule" poem may have as many lines as the writer likes).
2. Limitation of characters in each line (five or seven).
3. Observation of the tone pattern (the five-character four-line poems in old times did not observe this rule strictly).
4. Parallelism of the nature of words in each couplet (though the first and the last couplets may be exempted).
5. Selection of a single rhyme from the even tones and rhyming the last characters of alternate lines (the second, the fourth, the sixth, and the eighth lines; sometimes the first line also). The five-character four-line poems in the old days, however, were allowed rhymes from the uneven tones.
6. Avoidance of using a character twice unless deliberately repeated for effect.

Thus we see the great difficulty in writing a "modern" poem. But poets have always believed that the "modern" poem, though difficult to learn, is easy to write, while the "ancient" poem, though easy to learn, is very difficult to write well. Besides, the "modern" poem is constructed in a very convenient length. It enables the poet to finish his whole work while his thought is still fresh and inspiring; and, if necessary, he can express it in a series, either connected or separated. We find, ever since the T'ang Dynasty, most of the poets writing most of their poems in the "modern" forms.

Chinese Poetry in General

All the above statements treat only poems which are in Chinese called *shih*. This word is too narrow to correspond to the English word " poetry," which is more like the Chinese word " *yün-wên*," or rhythmic literature, and yet " *yün-wên* " has a broader content, for it includes also drama. There are, however, many other kinds of *yün-wên* besides *shih*, not only drama, but poetry in general. I will give a brief explanation of each; my idea being that the works we present in this volume, though the most common type of Chinese poetry, are but one of many types.

In the later part of the Chou Dynasty two new types of poetry were originated; one is the *ch'u-ts'ŭ*, by Ch'ü Yüan (fourth century, B.C.), and the other *fu*, by Hsün K'uang (fourth century B.C.). They are both, though rhymed, called rhythmic prose, and have been much practised ever since. The latter is more popular and used to be a subject in the official examinations. Since the Han Dynasty, the *yüeh-fu*, or poem " written for music," has been introduced into literature. We have a few examples in this volume in different forms. Because we do not sing them with their old music, which has vanished, they have practically lost their original quality, though still distinguished by title and style.

Another type of poetry, named *ts'ŭ*, was formulated in the second period of the T'ang Dynasty, but was not commonly practised until the last, or fourth, period. The Sung Dynasty is the golden age of the *ts'ŭ* poems and Li Ch'ing-chao and Chu Shu-chêng, two woman poets, are the most famous specialists. This form is composed of lines irregular, but according to fixed patterns. There are hundreds of patterns, each regulated as to the number of characters, group of tones, etc. In the same dynasty the *ch'ü*, or dramatic song, the *t'an-ts'ŭ*, or string song, and the *ku-shu*, or drum tale, were also brought into existence. The next dynasty, the Yüan or Mongol Dynasty, is known as the golden age of these forms of literature. Professional story-tellers or readers are found everywhere singing them with string instruments or drums. Besides these, the *ch'uan-ch'i*, or classical play, the *chiao-pên*, or common play, and the *hsiao-tiao*, or folk-song, are all very popular.

There are numberless Chinese poems written in the revolving order, to be read back and forth. The most amazing poems in human history are the *Huêi-wên-t'ü* or the revolving chart, by Lady Su Huêi, of the Chin Dynasty (265–419), and the *Ch'ien-tzŭ-wên*, or thousand-character literature, by Chou Hsing-ssŭ, (fifth century A.D.) The former is composed of eight hundred characters, originally woven in five colors on a piece of silk, being a love-poem written and sent to her husband, General Tou T'ao, who was then guarding the northern boundary against the Tartar invasion. The characters can be read from different ends in different directions and so form numerous poems. Four hundred have already been found, some short and some very long. It is believed that there are still more undiscovered. The latter, made of a thousand different characters, was a collection of stone inscriptions left by the master calligrapher, Wang Hsi-chih. They had been but loose characters in no order and with no connexion, but were arranged and rhymed as a perfect poem by Chou Hsing-ssŭ. The same thousand characters have been made into poems by ten or more authors; and these marvels in the poetical world can never be dreamed of by people who speak language other than Chinese!

All these various forms under various names are not *shih* in the Chinese sense, but are poetry in the English sense. Each of them possesses its own footing in the common ground of Chinese poetry. To make any remarks on Chinese poetry at large, or to draw any conclusions from it, one must take into consideration not only the *shih,* but all the various forms. I sometimes hear foreigners, as well as young Chinese students, blaming Chinese poems as being too stiff or confined. They do not realize that some forms of Chinese poetry are even freer than English free verse. They also criticize the Chinese for having no long poems, as other races have, ignoring the fact that many *fu* poems are thousands of lines long, with tens of thousands of characters, and that many rhythmic historical tales fill ten or more volumes, each volume following a single rhyme.

KIANG KANG-HU

Peking, China

THREE HUNDRED POEMS OF THE
T'ANG DYNASTY
618–906

Anonymous

氏名無

THE DAY OF NO FIRE

As the holiday approaches, and grasses are bright after rain,
And the causeway gleams with willows, and wheatfields wave in
    the wind,
We are thinking of our kinsfolk, far away from us.
O cuckoo, why do you follow us, why do you call us home?

(1, 1a)

Chang Chi

張 繼

A NIGHT-MOORING NEAR MAPLE BRIDGE

While I watch the moon go down, a crow caws through the frost;
Under the shadows of maple-trees a fisherman moves with his
    torch;
And I hear, from beyond Su-chou, from the temple on Cold
    Mountain,
Ringing for me, here in my boat, the midnight bell.

Chang Chi

籍 張

THINKING OF A FRIEND
LOST IN THE TIBETAN WAR

Last year you went with your troops to Tibet;
And when your men had vanished beyond the city-wall,
News was cut off between the two worlds
As between the living and the dead.
No one has come upon a faithful horse guarding
A crumpled tent or torn flag, or any trace of you.
If only I knew, I might serve you in the temple,
Instead of these tears toward the far sky.

Chang Ch'iao
喬 張

ON THE BORDER

Though a bugle breaks the crystal air of autumn,
Soldiers, in the look-out, watch at ease today
The spring wind blowing across green graves
And the pale sun setting beyond Liang-chou.
For now, on grey plains done with war,
The border is open to travel again;
And Tartars can no more choose than rivers:
They are running, all of them, toward the south.

Ch'ang Chien
建 常

A BUDDHIST RETREAT
BEHIND BROKEN-MOUNTAIN TEMPLE

In the pure morning, near the old temple,
Where early sunlight points the tree-tops,
My path has wound, through a sheltered hollow
Of boughs and flowers, to a Buddhist retreat.
Here birds are alive with mountain-light,
And the mind of man touches peace in a pool,
And a thousand sounds are quieted
By the breathing of a temple-bell.

AT WANG CH'ANG-LING'S RETREAT

Here, beside a clear deep lake,
You live accompanied by clouds;
Or soft through the pine the moon arrives
To be your own pure-hearted friend.
You rest under thatch in the shadow of your flowers,
Your dewy herbs flourish in their bed of moss.
Let me leave the world. Let me alight, like you,
On your western mountain with phœnixes and cranes.

Chang Chiu-ling

齡九張

LOOKING AT THE MOON
AND THINKING OF ONE FAR AWAY

The moon, grown full now over the sea,
Brightening the whole of heaven,
Brings to separated hearts
The long thoughtfulness of night. . . .
It is no darker though I blow out my candle.
It is no warmer though I put on my coat.
So I leave my message with the moon
And turn to my bed, hoping for dreams.

ORCHID AND ORANGE
(*A Plea for Official Preferment*)

I

Tender orchid-leaves in spring
And cinnamon-blossoms bright in autumn
Are as self-contained as life is,
Which conforms them to the seasons.

Yet why will you think that a forest-hermit,
Allured by sweet winds and contented with beauty,
Would no more ask to be transplanted
Than would any other natural flower?

II

Here, south of the Yang-tsze, grows a red orange-tree.
All winter long its leaves are green,
Not because of a warmer soil,
But because its nature is used to the cold.
Though it might serve your honourable guests,
You leave it here, far below mountain and river.
Circumstance governs destiny.
Cause and effect are an infinite cycle.
You plant your peach-trees and your plums,
You forget the shade from this other tree.

Chang Hsü

旭 張

PEACH-BLOSSOM RIVER

A bridge flies away through a wild mist,
Yet here are the rocks and the fisherman's boat.
Oh, if only this river of floating peach-petals
Might lead me at last to the mythical cave!

(2)

Chang Hu
祜　張

SHE SINGS AN OLD SONG

A lady of the palace these twenty years,
She has lived here a thousand miles from her home —
Yet ask her for this song and, with the first few words of it,
See how she tries to hold back her tears.

(3)

ON THE TERRACE OF ASSEMBLED ANGELS

I

The sun has gone slanting over a lordly roof
And red-blossoming branches have leaned toward the dew
Since the Emperor last night summoned a new favourite
And Lady Yang's bright smile came through the curtains.

II

The Emperor has sent for Lady Kuo Kuo.
In the morning, riding toward the palace-gate,
Disdainful of the paint that might have marred her beauty,
To meet him she smooths her two moth-tiny eyebrows.

(4)

OF ONE IN THE FORBIDDEN CITY

When the moonlight, reaching a tree by the gate,
Shows her a quiet bird on its nest,
She removes her jade hairpins and sits in the shadow
And puts out a flame where a moth was flying.

AT NAN-KING FERRY

This one-story inn at Nan-king ferry
Is a miserable lodging-place for the night —
But across the dead moon's ebbing tide,
Lights from Kua-chou beckon on the river.

Chang Pi

泌 張

A MESSAGE

I go in a dream to the house of Hsieh —
Through a zigzag porch with arching rails
To a court where the spring moon lights for ever
Phantom flowers and a single figure.

Ch'ên T'ao

吹 鄭

TURKESTAN

Thinking only of their vow that they would crush the Tartars —
On the desert, clad in sable and silk, five thousand of them fell. . . .
But arisen from their crumbling bones on the banks of the river
    at the border,
Dreams of them enter, like men alive, into rooms where their
    loves lie sleeping.

Ch'ên Tzŭ-ang
昂子陳

ON A GATE-TOWER AT YU-CHOU

Where, before me, are the ages that have gone?
And where, behind me, are the coming generations?
I think of heaven and earth, without limit, without end,
And I am all alone and my tears fall down.

Chêng T'ien

陶 陳

ON MA-WÊI SLOPE

When the Emperor came back from his ride, they had murdered
    Lady Yang —
That passion unforgettable through all the suns and moons.
They had led him to forsake her by reminding him
Of an emperor slain with his lady once, in a well at Ching-yang
    Palace.

(4, 4a)

Chia Tao

島 買

A NOTE LEFT FOR AN ABSENT RECLUSE

When I questioned your pupil, under a pine-tree,
" My teacher," he answered, " went for herbs,
But toward which corner of the mountain,
How can I tell, through all these clouds? "

Ch'ien Ch'i

起 錢

FAREWELL TO A JAPANESE BUDDHIST PRIEST
BOUND HOMEWARD

You were foreordained to find the source.
Now, tracing your way as in a dream
There where the sea floats up the sky,
You wane from the world in your fragile boat. . . .
The water and the moon are as calm as your faith,
Fishes and dragons follow your chanting,
And the eye still watches beyond the horizon
The holy light of your single lantern.

(5, 5a)

FROM MY STUDY AT THE MOUTH
OF THE VALLEY
A MESSAGE TO CENSOR YANG

At a little grass-hut in the valley of the river,
Where a cloud seems born from a viney wall,
You will love the bamboos new with rain,
And mountains tender in the sunset.

Cranes drift early here to rest
And autumn flowers are slow to fade. . . .
I have bidden my pupil to sweep the grassy path
For the coming of my friend.

TO MY FRIEND AT THE CAPITAL
SECRETARY P'AI

Finches flash yellow through the Imperial Grove
Of the Forbidden City, pale with spring dawn;
Flowers muffle a bell in the Palace of Bliss
And rain has deepened the Dragon Lake willows;
But spring is no help to a man bewildered,
Who would be like a cloud upholding the Light of Heaven,
Yet whose poems, ten years refused, are shaming
These white hairs held by the petalled pin.

(6, 7)

Chin Ch'ang-hsü

緒昌金

A SPRING SIGH

Drive the orioles away,
All their music from the trees. . . .
When she dreamed that she went to Liao-hsi Camp
To join him there, they wakened her.

Ch'in T'ao-yü
玉韜秦

A POOR GIRL

Living under a thatch roof, never wearing fragrant silk,
She longs to arrange a marriage, but how could she dare?
Who would know her simple face the loveliest of them all
When we choose for worldliness, not for worth?
Her fingers embroider beyond compare,
But she cannot vie with painted brows;
And year after year she has sewn gold thread
On bridal robes for other girls.

Ch'iu Wêi
爲 邱

AFTER MISSING THE RECLUSE
ON THE WESTERN MOUNTAIN

To your hermitage here on the top of the mountain
I have climbed, without stopping, these ten miles.
I have knocked at your door, and no one answered;
I have peeped into your room, at your seat beside the table.
Perhaps you are out riding in your canopied chair,
Or fishing, more likely, in some autumn pool.
Sorry though I am to be missing you,
You have become my meditation —
The beauty of your grasses, fresh with rain,
And close beside your window the music of your pines.
I take into my being all that I see and hear,
Soothing my senses, quieting my heart;
And though there be neither host nor guest,
Have I not reasoned a visit complete?
. . . After enough, I have gone down the mountain.
Why should I wait for you any longer?

Chi-wu Ch'ien

潛毋綦

A BOAT IN SPRING ON JO-YA LAKE

Thoughtful elation has no end:
Onward I bear it to whatever come.
And my boat and I, before the evening breeze
Passing flowers, entering the lake,
Turn at nightfall toward the western valley,
Where I watch the south star over the mountain
And a mist that rises, hovering soft,
And the low moon slanting through the trees;
And I choose to put away from me every worldly matter
And only to be an old man with a fishing-pole.

Chu Ch'ing-yü

餘慶朱

A SONG OF THE PALACE

Now that the palace-gate has softly closed on its flowers,
Ladies file out to their pavilion of jade,
Abrim to the lips with imperial gossip
But not daring to breathe it with a parrot among them.

ON THE EVE OF GOVERNMENT EXAMINATIONS
To Secretary Chang

Out go the great red wedding-chamber candles.
Tomorrow in state the bride faces your parents.
She has finished preparing; she asks of you meekly
Whether her eyebrows are painted in fashion.

(72)

Ch'üan Tê-yü

輿德權

THE JADE DRESSING-TABLE

Last night my girdle came undone,
And this morning a luck-beetle flew over my bed.
So here are my paints and here are my powders —
And a welcome for my yoke again.

(8)

Han Hung

韓 翃

AFTER THE DAY OF NO FIRE

Petals of spring fly all through the city
From the wind in the willows of the Imperial River.
And at dusk, from the palace, candles are given out
To light first the mansions of the Five Great Lords.

(1)

AN AUTUMN EVENING
HARMONIZING CH'ÊNG CHIN'S POEM

While a cold wind is creeping under my mat,
And the city's naked wall grows pale with the autumn moon,
I see a lone wildgoose crossing the River of Stars,
And I hear, on stone in the night, thousands of washing-
 mallets. . . .
But, instead of wishing the season, as it goes,
To bear me also far away,
I have found your poem so beautiful
That I forget the homing birds.

(9, 10)

INSCRIBED
IN THE TEMPLE OF THE WANDERING GENIE

I face, high over this enchanted lodge, the Court of the Five Cities
    of Heaven,
And I see a countryside blue and still, after the long rain.
The distant peaks and trees of Ch'in merge into twilight,
And Han Palace washing-stones make their autumnal echoes.
Thin pine-shadows brush the outdoor pulpit,
And grasses blow their fragrance into my little cave.
. . . Who need be craving a world beyond this one?
Here, among men, are the Purple Hills!

(10, 11)

Han Wu

偓 韓

COOLER WEATHER

Her jade-green alcove curtained thick with silk,
Her vermilion screen with its pattern of flowers,
Her eight-foot dragon-beard mat and her quilt brocaded in squares
Are ready now for nights that are neither warm nor cold.

(12)

Han Yü
愈 韓

MOUNTAIN-STONES

Rough were the mountain-stones, and the path very narrow;
And when I reached the temple, bats were in the dusk.
I climbed to the hall, sat on the steps, and drank the rain-washed
    air
Among the round gardenia-pods and huge banana-leaves.
On the old wall, said the priest, were Buddhas finely painted,
And he brought a light and showed me, and I called them won-
    derful.
He spread the bed, dusted the mats, and made my supper ready,
And, though the food was coarse, it satisfied my hunger.
At midnight, while I lay there not hearing even an insect,
The mountain moon with her pure light entered my door. . . .
At dawn I left the mountain and, alone, lost my way:
In and out, up and down, while a heavy mist
Made brook and mountain green and purple, brightening every-
    thing.
I am passing sometimes pines and oaks, which ten men could
    not girdle,
I am treading pebbles barefoot in swift-running water —
Its ripples purify my ear, while a soft wind blows my gar-
    ments. . . .

These are the things which, in themselves, make life happy.
Why should we be hemmed about and hampered with people?
O chosen pupils, far behind me in my own country,
What if I spent my old age here and never went back home?

ON THE FESTIVAL OF THE MOON

To Sub-Official Chang

The fine clouds have opened and the River of Stars is gone,
A clear wind blows across the sky, and the moon widens its wave,
The sand is smooth, the water still, no sound and no shadow,
As I offer you a cup of wine, asking you to sing.
But so sad is this song of yours and so bitter your voice
That before I finish listening my tears have become a rain:
"Where Lake Tung-t'ing is joined to the sky by the lofty Nine-
    Doubt Mountain,
Dragons, crocodiles, rise and sink, apes, flying foxes, whimper. . . .
At a ten to one risk of death, I have reached my official post,
Where lonely I live and hushed, as though I were in hiding.
I leave my bed, afraid of snakes; I eat, fearing poisons;
The air of the lake is putrid, breathing its evil odours. . . .
Yesterday, by the district office, the great drum was announcing
The crowning of an emperor, a change in the realm.
The edict granting pardons runs three hundred miles a day,
All those who were to die have had their sentences commuted,
The unseated are promoted and exiles are recalled,

Corruptions are abolished, clean officers appointed.
My superior sent my name in. but the governor would not listen
And has only transferred me to this barbaric place.
My rank is very low and useless to refer to;
They might punish me with lashes in the dust of the street.
Most of my fellow exiles are now returning home —
A journey which, to me, is a heaven beyond climbing."
. . . Stop your song, I beg you, and listen to mine,
A song that is utterly different from yours:
" Tonight is the loveliest moon of the year.
All else is with fate, not ours to control;
But, refusing this wine, may we choose more tomorrow? "

STOPPING AT A TEMPLE ON HÊNG MOUNTAIN
I INSCRIBE THIS POEM IN THE GATE-TOWER

The five Holy Mountains have the rank of the Three Dukes.
The other four make a ring, with the Sung Mountain midmost.
To this one, in the fire-ruled south, where evil signs are rife,
Heaven gave divine power, ordaining it a peer.
All the clouds and hazes are hidden in its girdle;
And its forehead is beholden only by a few.
. . . I came here in autumn, during the rainy season,
When the sky was overcast and the clear wind gone.
I quieted my mind and prayed, hoping for an answer;
For assuredly righteous thinking reaches to high heaven.
And soon all the mountain-peaks were showing me their faces;

I looked up at a pinnacle that held the clean blue sky:
The wide Purple Canopy joined the Celestial Column;
The Stone Granary leapt, while the Fire God stood still.
Moved by this token, I dismounted to offer thanks.
A long path of pine and cypress led to the temple.
Its white walls and purple pillars shone, and the vivid colour
Of gods and devils filled the place with patterns of red and blue.
I climbed the steps and, bending down to sacrifice, besought
That my pure heart might be welcome, in spite of my humble
    offering.
The old priest professed to know the judgment of the God:
He was polite and reverent, making many bows.
He handed me divinity-cups, he showed me how to use them
And told me that my fortune was the very best of all.
Though exiled to a barbarous land, mine is a happy life.
Plain food and plain clothes are all I ever wanted.
To be prince, duke, premier, general, was never my desire;
And if the God would bless me, what better could he grant than
    this? —
At night I lie down to sleep in the top of a high tower;
While moon and stars glimmer through the darkness of the
    clouds. . . .
Apes call, a bell sounds. And ready for dawn,
I see arise, far in the east, the cold bright sun.

(13, 13a, 14, 14a)

A POEM ON THE STONE DRUMS

Chang handed me this tracing, from the stone drums,
Beseeching me to write a poem on the stone drums.
Tu Fu has gone. Li Po is dead.
What can my poor talent do for the stone drums?
. . . When the Chou power waned and China was bubbling,
Emperor Hsüan, up in wrath, waved his holy spear
And opened his Great Audience, receiving all the tributes
Of kings and lords who came to him with a tune of clanging
    weapons.
They held a hunt in Ch'i-yang and proved their marksmanship:
Fallen birds and animals were strewn three thousand miles.
And the exploit was recorded, to inform new generations. . . .
Cut out of jutting cliffs, these drums made of stone —
On which poets and artisans, all of the first order,
Had indited and chiselled — were set in the deep mountains
To be washed by rain, baked by sun, burned by wildfire,
Eyed by evil spirits, and protected by the gods.
. . . Where can he have found the tracing on this paper? —
True to the original, not altered by a hair,
The meaning deep, the phrases cryptic, difficult to read,
And the style of the characters neither square nor tadpole.
Time has not yet vanquished the beauty of these letters —
Looking like sharp daggers that pierce live crocodiles,
Like phœnix-mates dancing, like angels hovering down,
Like trees of jade and coral with interlocking branches,
Like golden cord and iron chain tied together tight,

Like incense-tripods flung in the sea, like dragons mounting
    heaven.
Historians, gathering ancient poems, forgot to gather these,
To make the two Books of Musical Song more colourful and
    striking;
Confucius journeyed in the west, but not to the Ch'in Kingdom,
He chose our planet and our stars but missed the sun and
    moon. . . .
I who am fond of antiquity, was born too late
And, thinking of these wonderful things, cannot hold back my
    tears . . .
I remember, when I was awarded my highest degree,
During the first year of Yüan-ho,
How a friend of mine, then at the western camp,
Offered to assist me in removing these old relics.
I bathed and changed, then made my plea to the college president
And urged on him the rareness of these most precious things.
They could be wrapped in rugs, be packed and sent in boxes
And carried on only a few camels: ten stone drums
To grace the Imperial Temple like the Incense-Pot of Kao —
Or their lustre and their value would increase a hundredfold,
If the monarch would present them to the university,
Where students could study them and doubtless decipher them,
And multitudes, attracted to the capital of culture
From all corners of the Empire, would be quick to gather.
We could scour the moss, pick out the dirt, restore the original
    surface,
And lodge them in a fitting and secure place for ever,
Covered by a massive building with wide eaves

Where nothing more might happen to them as it had before.
. . . But government officials grow fixed in their ways
And never will initiate beyond old precedent;
So herd-boys strike the drums for fire, cows polish horns on them,
With no one to handle them reverentially.
Still ageing and decaying, soon they may be effaced.
Six years I have sighed for them, chanting toward the west. . . .
The familiar script of Wang Hsi-chih, beautiful though it was,
Could be had, several pages, just for a few white geese!
But now, eight dynasties after the Chou, and all the wars over,
Why should there be nobody caring for these drums?
The Empire is at peace, the government free.
Poets again are honoured and Confucians and Mencians. . . .
Oh, how may this petition be carried to the throne?
It needs indeed an eloquent flow, like a cataract —
But, alas, my voice has broken, in my song of the stone drums,
To a sound of supplication choked with its own tears.

(15, 16)

Hê Chih-chang

章知賀

COMING HOME

I left home young. I return old,
Speaking as then, but with hair grown thin;
And my children, meeting me, do not know me.
They smile and say: "Stranger, where do you come from?"

(17)

Hsü Hun

許 渾

INSCRIBED IN THE INN AT T'UNG GATE ON AN AUTUMN TRIP TO THE CAPITAL

Red leaves are fluttering down the twilight
Past this arbour where I take my wine;
Cloud-rifts are blowing toward Great Flower Mountain,
And a shower is crossing the Middle Ridge.
I can see trees colouring a distant wall.
I can hear the river seeking the sea,
As I the Imperial City tomorrow —
But I dream of woodsmen and fishermen.

(14)

EARLY AUTUMN

There's a harp in the midnight playing clear,
While the west wind rustles a green vine;
There's a low cloud touching the jade-white dew
And an early wildgoose in the River of Stars. . . .

Night in the tall trees clings to dawn;
Light makes folds in the distant hills;
And here on the Huai, by one falling leaf,
I can feel a storm on Lake Tung-t'ing.

(18)

Emperor Hsüan-tsung (Ming Huang)

宗 玄

I PASS THROUGH THE LU DUKEDOM
WITH A SIGH AND A SACRIFICE FOR CONFUCIUS

O Master, how did the world repay
Your life of long solicitude? —
The Lords of Tsou have misprized your land,
And your home has been used as the palace of Lu. . . .
You foretold that when phœnixes vanished, your fortunes too
    would end,
You knew that the captured unicorn would be a sign of the close
    of your teaching. . . .
Can this sacrifice I watch, here between two temple-pillars,
Be the selfsame omen of death you dreamed of long ago?

(4a, c, d, 19, 19a)

Hsüeh Fêng

逢 薛

A PALACE POEM

In twelve chambers the ladies, decked for the day,
Peer afar for their lord from their Fairy-View Lodge;
The golden toad guards the lock on the door-chain,
And the bronze-dragon water-clock drips through the morn-
    ing —
Till one of them, tilting a mirror, combs her cloud of hair
And chooses new scent and a change of silk raiment;
For she sees, between screen-panels, deep in the palace,
Eunuchs in court-dress preparing a bed.

Huang-fu Jan

皇甫冉

SPRING THOUGHTS

Finch-notes and swallow-notes tell the new year . . .
But so far are the Town of the Horse and the Dragon Mound
From this our house, from these walls and Han Gardens,
That the moon takes my heart to the Tartar sky.
I have woven in the frame endless words of my grieving . . .
Yet this petal-bough is smiling now on my lonely sleep.
. . . Oh, ask General Tou when his flags will come home
And his triumph be carved on the rock of Yen-jan Mountain!

(20)

Kao Shih

高 適

TO VICE-PREFECTS LI AND WANG
DEGRADED AND TRANSFERRED
TO HSIA-CHUNG AND CH'ANG-SHA

What are you thinking as we part from one another,
Pulling in our horses for the stirrup-cups?
Do these tear-streaks mean Wu Valley monkeys all weeping,
Or wildgeese returning with news from Hêng Mountain? . . .
On the river between green maples an autumn sail grows dim,
There are only a few old trees by the wall of the White God
    City . . .
But the year is bound to freshen us with a dew of heavenly
    favour —
Take heart, we shall soon be together again!

(21, 14)

A SONG OF THE YEN COUNTRY
(*Written to Music*)

(*In the sixth year of K'ai-yüan, a friend returned from the border and showed me the Yen Song. Moved by what he told me of the expedition, I have written this poem to the same rhymes.*)

The northeastern border of China was dark with smoke and dust.
To repel the savage invaders, our generals, leaving their families,
Strode forth together, looking as heroes should look;
And having received from the Emperor his most gracious favour,
They marched to the beat of gong and drum through the Elm
Pass.
They circled the Stone Tablet with a line of waving flags,
Till their captains over the Sea of Sand were twanging feathered
orders.
The Tartar chieftain's hunting-fires glimmered along Wolf
Mountain,
And heights and rivers were cold and bleak there at the outer
border;
But soon the barbarians' horses were plunging through wind
and rain.
Half of our men at the front were killed, but the other half are
living,
And still at the camp beautiful girls dance for them and sing.
. . . As autumn ends in the grey sand, with the grasses all
withered,
The few surviving watchers by the lonely wall at sunset,

Serving in a good cause, hold life and the foeman lightly.
And yet, for all that they have done, Elm Pass is still unsafe.
Still at the front, iron armour is worn and battered thin,
And here at home food-sticks are made of jade tears.
Still in this southern city young wives' hearts are breaking,
While soldiers at the northern border vainly look toward home.
The fury of the wind cuts our men's advance
In a place of death and blue void, with nothingness ahead.
Three times a day a cloud of slaughter rises over the camp;
And all night long the hour-drums shake their chilly booming,
Until white swords can be seen again, spattered with red blood.
. . . When death becomes a duty, who stops to think of fame?
Yet in speaking of the rigours of warfare on the desert
We name to this day Li, the great General, who lived long ago.

(22)

Ku K'uang

況 顧

A PALACE POEM

High above, from a jade chamber, songs float half-way to heaven,
The palace-girls' gay voices are mingled with the wind —
But now they are still, and you hear a water-clock drip in the
    Court of the Moon. . . .
They have opened the curtain wide, they are facing the River of
    Stars.

Li Ch'i

顧 李

A FAREWELL TO WÊI WAN
BOUND FOR THE CAPITAL

The travellers' parting-song sounds in the dawn.
Last night a first frost came over the river;
And the crying of the wildgeese grieves my sad heart
Bounded by a gloom of cloudy mountains. . . .
Here in the Gate City, day will flush cold
And washing-flails quicken by the gardens at twilight —
How long shall the capital content you,
Where the months and the years so vainly go by?

(23)

AN OLD AIR

There once was a man, sent on military missions,
A wanderer, from youth, on the Yu and Yen frontiers.
Under the horses' hoofs he would meet his foes
And, recklessly risking his seven-foot body,
Would slay whoever dared confront
Those moustaches that bristled like porcupine-quills.

. . . There were dark clouds below the hills, there were white
    clouds above them,
But before a man has served full time, how can he go back?
In eastern Liao a girl was waiting, a girl of fifteen years,
Deft with a guitar, expert in dance and song.
. . . She seems to be fluting, even now, a reed-song of home,
Filling every soldier's eyes with homesick tears.

A FAREWELL TO MY FRIEND CH'ÊN CHANG-FU

In the Fourth-month the south wind blows plains of yellow barley,
Date-flowers have not faded yet and lakka-leaves are long.
The green peak that we left at dawn we still can see at evening,
While our horses whinny on the road, eager to turn homeward.
. . . Ch'ên, my friend, you have always been a great and good
    man,
With your dragon's moustache, tiger's eyebrows and your massive
    forehead.
In your bosom you have shelved away ten thousand volumes.
You have held your head high, never bowed it in the dust.
. . . After buying us wine and pledging us, here at the east-
    ern gate,
And taking things as lightly as a wildgoose feather,
Flat you lie, tipsy, forgetting the white sun;
But now and then you open your eyes and gaze at a high lone
    cloud.
. . . The tide-head of the long river joins the darkening sky.

The ferryman beaches his boat. It has grown too late to sail.
And people on their way from Chêng cannot go home,
And people from Lo-yang sigh with disappointment.
. . . I have heard about the many friends around your wood-
land dwelling.
Yesterday you were dismissed. Are they your friends today?

A LUTE SONG

Our host, providing abundant wine to make the night mellow,
Asks his guest from Yang-chou to play for us on the lute.
Toward the moon that whitens the city-wall, black crows are fly-
ing,
Frost is on ten thousand trees, and the wind blows through our
clothes;
But a copper stove has added its light to that of flowery candles,
And the lute plays *The Green Water,* and then *The Queen of Ch'u.*
Once it has begun to play, there is no other sound:
A spell is on the banquet, while the stars grow thin. . . .
But three hundred miles from here, in Huai, official duties await
him,
And so it's farewell, and the road again, under cloudy mountains.

ON HEARING TUNG PLAY THE FLAGEOLET
A POEM TO PALACE-ATTENDANT FANG

When this melody for the flageolet was made by Lady Ts'ai,
When long ago one by one she sang its eighteen stanzas,
Even the Tartars were shedding tears into the border-grasses,
And the envoy of China was heart-broken, turning back home
    with his escort.
. . . Cold fires now of old battles are grey on ancient forts,
And the wilderness is shadowed with white new-flying snow.
. . . When the player first brushes the Shang string and the
    Chüeh and then the Yü,
Autumn-leaves in all four quarters are shaken with a murmur.
Tung, the master,
Must have been taught in heaven.
Demons come from the deep pine-wood and stealthily listen
To music slow, then quick, following his hand,
Now far away, now near again, according to his heart.
A hundred birds from an empty mountain scatter and return;
Three thousand miles of floating clouds darken and lighten;
A wildgoose fledgling, left behind, cries for its flock,
And a Tartar child for the mother he loves.
Then river waves are calmed
And birds are mute that were singing,
And Wu-chu tribes are homesick for their distant land,
And out of the dust of Siberian steppes rises a plaintive sorrow.
. . . Suddenly the low sound leaps to a freer tune,
Like a long wind swaying a forest, a downpour breaking tiles,

A cascade through the air, flying over tree-tops.

. . . A wild deer calls to his fellows. He is running among the
 mansions

In the corner of the capital by the Eastern Palace wall . . .

Phœnix Lake lies opposite the Gate of Green Jade;

But how can fame and profit concern a man of genius?

Day and night I long for him to bring his lute again.

(23)

ON HEARING AN WAN-SHAN PLAY THE
REED-PIPE

Bamboo from the southern hills was used to make this pipe.

And its music, that was introduced from Persia first of all,

Has taken on new magic through later use in China.

And now the Tartar from Liang-chou, blowing it for me,

Drawing a sigh from whosoever hears it,

Is bringing to a wanderer's eyes homesick tears. . . .

Many like to listen; but few understand.

To and fro at will there's a long wind flying,

Dry mulberry-trees, old cypresses, trembling in its chill.

There are nine baby phœnixes, outcrying one another;

A dragon and a tiger spring up at the same moment;

Then in a hundred waterfalls ten thousand songs of autumn

Are suddenly changing to *The Yü-yang Lament;*

And when yellow clouds grow thin and the white sun darkens,

They are changing still again to *Spring in the Willow-Trees*.
Like Imperial Garden flowers, brightening the eye with beauty,
Are the high-hall candles we have lighted this cold night,
And with every cup of wine goes another round of music.

AN OLD WAR-SONG

(*Written to Music*)

Through the bright day up the mountain, we scan the sky for a
    war-torch;
At yellow dusk we water our horses in the boundary-river;
And when the throb of watch-drums hangs in the sandy wind,
We hear the guitar of the Chinese Princess telling her endless
    woe. . . .
Three thousand miles without a town, nothing but camps,
Till the heavy sky joins the wide desert in snow.
With their plaintive calls, barbarian wildgeese fly from night to
    night,
And children of the Tartars have many tears to shed;
But we hear that the Jade Pass is still under siege,
And soon we stake our lives upon our light war-chariots.
Each year we bury in the desert bones unnumbered,
Yet we only watch for grape-vines coming into China.

(24, 25)

Li P'in

頻 李

CROSSING THE HAN RIVER

Away from home, I was longing for news
Winter after winter, spring after spring.
Now, nearing my village, meeting people,
I dare not ask a single question.

Li Po

白 李

IN THE QUIET NIGHT

So bright a gleam on the foot of my bed —
Could there have been a frost already?
Lifting myself to look, I found that it was moonlight.
Sinking back again, I thought suddenly of home.

A BITTER LOVE

How beautiful she looks, opening the pearly casement,
And how quiet she leans, and how troubled her brow is!
You may see the tears now, bright on her cheek,
But not the man she so bitterly loves.

A SIGH FROM A STAIRCASE OF JADE
(*Written to Music*)

Her jade-white staircase is cold with dew;
Her silk soles are wet, she lingered there so long . . .
Behind her closed casement, why is she still waiting,
Watching through its crystal pane the glow of the autumn moon?

(27)

A FAREWELL TO MĔNG HAO-JAN
ON HIS WAY TO YANG-CHOU

You have left me behind, old friend, at the Yellow Crane Terrace,
On your way to visit Yang-chou in the misty month of flowers;
Your sail, a single shadow, becomes one with the blue sky,
Till now I see only the river, on its way to heaven.

(28, 28a)

THROUGH THE YANG-TSZE GORGES

From the walls of Po-ti high in the coloured dawn
To Kiang-ling by night-fall is three hundred miles,
Yet monkeys are still calling on both banks behind me
To my boat these ten thousand mountains away.

(29)

A SONG OF PURE HAPPINESS
(*Written to Music for Lady Yang*)

I

Her robe is a cloud, her face a flower;
Her balcony, glimmering with the bright spring dew,
Is either the tip of earth's Jade Mountain
Or a moon-edged roof of paradise.

II

There's a perfume stealing moist from a shaft of red blossom,
And a mist, through the heart, from the magical Hill of Wu —
The palaces of China have never known such beauty —
Not even Flying Swallow with all her glittering garments.

III

Lovely now together, his lady and his flowers
Lighten for ever the Emperor's eye,
As he listens to the sighing of the far spring wind
Where she leans on a railing in the Aloe Pavilion.

(4, 4b, 26, 26a)

A MESSAGE TO MÊNG HAO-JAN

Master, I hail you from my heart,
And your fame arisen to the skies. . . .
Renouncing in ruddy youth the importance of hat and chariot,
You chose pine-trees and clouds; and now, white-haired,
Drunk with the moon, a sage of dreams,
Flower-bewitched, you are deaf to the Emperor . . .
High mountain, how I long to reach you,
Breathing your sweetness even here!

(32a)

BIDDING A FRIEND FAREWELL
AT CHING-MÊN FERRY

Sailing far off from Ching-mên Ferry,
Soon you will be with people in the south,
Where the mountains end and the plains begin
And the river winds through wilderness. . . .
The moon is lifted like a mirror,
Sea-clouds gleam like palaces,
And the water has brought you a touch of home
To draw your boat three hundred miles.

A FAREWELL TO A FRIEND

With a blue line of mountains north of the wall,
And east of the city a white curve of water,
Here you must leave me and drift away
Like a loosened water-plant hundreds of miles. . . .
I shall think of you in a floating cloud;
So in the sunset think of me.
. . . We wave our hands to say good-bye,
And my horse is neighing again and again.

ON HEARING CHÜN
THE BUDDHIST MONK FROM SHU
PLAY HIS LUTE

The monk from Shu with his green silk lute-case,
Walking west down O-mêi Mountain,
Has brought me by one touch of the strings
The breath of pines in a thousand valleys.
I hear him in the cleansing brook,
I hear him in the icy bells;
And I feel no change though the mountain darkens
And cloudy autumn heaps the sky.

THOUGHTS OF OLD TIME
FROM A NIGHT-MOORING
UNDER MOUNT NIU-CHU

This night to the west of the river-brim
There is not one cloud in the whole blue sky,
As I watch from my deck the autumn moon,
Vainly remembering old General Hsieh. . . .
I have poems; I can read;
He heard others, but not mine.
. . . Tomorrow I shall hoist my sail,
With fallen maple-leaves behind me.

(30)

ON CLIMBING IN NAN-KING
TO THE TERRACE OF PHŒNIXES

Phœnixes that played here once, so that the place was
    named for them,
Have abandoned it now to this desolate river;
The paths of Wu Palace are crooked with weeds;
The garments of Chin are ancient dust.
. . . Like this green horizon halving the Three Peaks,
Like this Island of White Egrets dividing the river,
A cloud has arisen between the Light of Heaven and me,
To hide his city from my melancholy heart.

(6, 31)

DOWN CHUNG-NAN MOUNTAIN
TO THE KIND PILLOW AND BOWL OF HU SSÜ

Down the blue mountain in the evening,
Moonlight was my homeward escort.
Looking back, I saw my path
Lie in levels of deep shadow . . .
I was passing the farm-house of a friend,
When his children called from a gate of thorn
And led me twining through jade bamboos
Where green vines caught and held my clothes.
And I was glad of a chance to rest
And glad of a chance to drink with my friend. . . .
We sang to the tune of the wind in the pines;
And we finished our songs as the stars went down,
When, I being drunk and my friend more than happy,
Between us we forgot the world.

(32)

DRINKING ALONE WITH THE MOON

From a pot of wine among the flowers
I drank alone. There was no one with me —
Till, raising my cup, I asked the bright moon
To bring me my shadow and make us three.
Alas, the moon was unable to drink

And my shadow tagged me vacantly;
But still for a while I had these friends
To cheer me through the end of spring. . . .
I sang. The moon encouraged me.
I danced. My shadow tumbled after.
As long as I knew, we were boon companions.
And then I was drunk, and we lost one another.
. . . . Shall goodwill ever be secure?
I watch the long road of the River of Stars.

IN SPRING

Your grasses up north are as blue as jade,
Our mulberries here curve green-threaded branches;
And at last you think of returning home,
Now when my heart is almost broken. . . .
O breeze of the spring, since I dare not know you,
Why part the silk curtains by my bed?

THE MOON AT THE FORTIFIED PASS
(Written to Music)

The bright moon lifts from the Mountain of Heaven
In an infinite haze of cloud and sea,
And the wind, that has come a thousand miles,

Beats at the Jade Pass battlements. . . .
China marches its men down Po-têng Road
While Tartar troops peer across blue waters of the bay . . .
And since not one battle famous in history
Sent all its fighters back again,
The soldiers turn round, looking toward the border,
And think of home, with wistful eyes,
And of those tonight in the upper chambers
Who toss and sigh and cannot rest.

A SONG OF AN AUTUMN MIDNIGHT
(*Written to a Su-chou Melody*)

A slip of the moon hangs over the capital;
Ten thousand washing-mallets are pounding;
And the autumn wind is blowing my heart
For ever and ever toward the Jade Pass. . . .
Oh, when will the Tartar troops be conquered,
And my husband come back from the long campaign!

A SONG OF CH'ANG-KAN
(*Written to Music*)

My hair had hardly covered my forehead.
I was picking flowers, playing by my door,

When you, my lover, on a bamboo horse,
Came trotting in circles and throwing green plums.
We lived near together on a lane in Ch'ang-kan,
Both of us young and happy-hearted.
. . . At fourteen I became your wife,
So bashful that I dared not smile,
And I lowered my head toward a dark corner
And would not turn to your thousand calls;
But at fifteen I straightened my brows and laughed,
Learning that no dust could ever seal our love,
That even unto death I would await you by my post
And would never lose heart in the tower of silent watching.
. . . Then when I was sixteen, you left on a long journey
Through the Gorges of Ch'ü-t'ang, of rock and whirling water.
And then came the Fifth-month, more than I could bear,
And I tried to hear the monkeys in your lofty far-off sky.
Your footprints by our door, where I had watched you go,
Were hidden, every one of them, under green moss,
Hidden under moss too deep to sweep away.
And the first autumn wind added fallen leaves.
And now, in the Eighth-month, yellowing butterflies
Hover, two by two, in our west-garden grasses. . . .
And, because of all this, my heart is breaking
And I fear for my bright cheeks, lest they fade.
. . . Oh, at last, when you return through the three Pa districts,
Send me a message home ahead!
And I will come and meet you and will never mind the distance,
All the way to Chang-fêng Sha.

(33)

A SONG OF LU MOUNTAIN
To Censor Lu Hsü-chou

I am the madman of the Ch'u country
Who sang a mad song disputing Confucius.
. . . Holding in my hand a staff of green jade,
I have crossed, since morning at the Yellow Crane Terrace,
All five Holy Mountains, without a thought of distance,
According to the one constant habit of my life.
. . . Lu Mountain stands beside the Southern Dipper
In clouds reaching silken like a nine-panelled screen,
With its shadows in a crystal lake deepening the green water.
The Golden Gate opens into two mountain-ranges.
A silver stream is hanging down to three stone bridges
Within sight of the mighty Tripod Falls.
Ledges of cliff and winding trails lead to blue sky
And a flush of cloud in the morning sun,
Whence no flight of birds could be blown into Wu.
. . . I climb to the top. I survey the whole world.
I see the long river that runs beyond return,
Yellow clouds that winds have driven hundreds of miles
And a snow-peak whitely circled by the swirl of a ninefold stream.
And so I am singing a song of Lu Mountain,
A song that is born of the breath of Lu Mountain.
. . . Where the Stone Mirror makes the heart's purity purer
And green moss has buried the footsteps of Hsieh,
I have eaten the immortal pellet and, rid of the world's troubles,
Before the lute's third playing have achieved my element.

Far away I watch the angels riding coloured clouds
Toward heaven's Jade City, with hibiscus in their hands.
And so, when I have traversed the nine sections of the world,
I will follow Saint Lu-ao up the Great Purity.

(14, 34, 34a)

T'IEN-MU MOUNTAIN ASCENDED IN A DREAM

A seafaring visitor will talk about Japan,
Which waters and mists conceal beyond approach;
But Yüeh people talk about Heavenly Mother Mountain,
Still seen through its varying deepnesses of cloud.
In a straight line to heaven, its summit enters heaven,
Tops the five Holy Peaks, and casts a shadow through China
With the hundred-mile length of the Heavenly Terrace Range,
Which, just at this point, begins turning southeast.
. . . My heart and my dreams are in Wu and Yüeh
And they cross Mirror Lake all night in the moon.
And the moon lights my shadow
And me to Yien River —
With the hermitage of Hsieh still there
And the monkeys calling clearly over ripples of green water.
I wear his pegged boots
Up a ladder of blue cloud,
Sunny ocean half-way,
Holy cock-crow in space,
Myriad peaks and more valleys and nowhere a road.

Flowers lure me, rocks ease me. Day suddenly ends.

Bears, dragons, tempestuous on mountain and river,

Startle the forest and make the heights tremble.

Clouds darken with darkness of rain,

Streams pale with pallor of mist.

The Gods of Thunder and Lightning

Shatter the whole range.

The stone gate breaks asunder

Venting in the pit of heaven,

An impenetrable shadow.

. . . But now the sun and moon illumine a gold and silver terrace,

And, clad in rainbow garments, riding on the wind,

Come the queens of all the clouds, descending one by one,

With tigers for their lute-players and phœnixes for dancers.

Row upon row, like fields of hemp, range the fairy figures. . . .

I move, my soul goes flying,

I wake with a long sigh,

My pillow and my matting

Are the lost clouds I was in.

. . . And this is the way it always is with human joy:

Ten thousand things run for ever like water toward the east.

And so I take my leave of you, not knowing for how long.

. . . But let me, on my green slope, raise a white deer

And ride to you, great mountain, when I have need of you.

Oh, how can I gravely bow and scrape to men of high rank and
    men of high office

Who never will suffer being shown an honest-hearted face!

(34a)

PARTING AT A WINE-SHOP IN NAN-KING

A wind, bringing willow-cotton, sweetens the shop,
And a girl from Wu, pouring wine, urges me to share it
With my comrades of the city who are here to see me off;
And as each of them drains his cup, I say to him in parting,
Oh, go and ask this river running to the east
If it can travel farther than a friend's love!

A FAREWELL TO SECRETARY SHU-YÜN
AT THE HSIEH T'IAO VILLA IN HSÜAN-CHOU

Since yesterday had to throw me and bolt,
Today has hurt my heart even more.
The autumn wildgeese have a long wind for escort
As I face them from this villa, drinking my wine.
The bones of great writers are your brushes, in the School of
      Heaven,
And I am a Lesser Hsieh growing up by your side.
We both are exalted to distant thought,
Aspiring to the sky and the bright moon.
But since water still flows, though we cut it with our swords,
And sorrows return, though we drown them with wine,
Since the world can in no way answer our craving,
I will loosen my hair tomorrow and take to a fishing-boat.

(35)

HARD ROADS IN SHU

(*Written to Music*)

Oh, but it is high and very dangerous!

Such travelling is harder than scaling the blue sky.

. . . Until two rulers of this region

Pushed their way through in the misty ages,

Forty-eight thousand years had passed

With nobody arriving across the Ch'in border.

And the Great White Mountain, westward, still has only a bird's
      path

Up to the summit of O-mêi Peak —

Which was broken once by an earthquake and there were brave
      men lost,

Just finishing the stone rungs of their ladder toward heaven.

. . . High, as on a tall flag, six dragons drive the sun,

While the river, far below, lashes its twisted course.

Such height would be hard going for even a yellow crane,

So pity the poor monkeys who have only paws to use.

The Mountain of Green Clay is formed of many circles —

Each hundred steps, we have to turn nine turns among its mounds.

Panting, we brush Orion and pass the Well Star,

Then, holding our chests with our hands and sinking to the
      ground with a groan,

We wonder if this westward trail will never have an end.

The formidable path ahead grows darker, darker still,

With nothing heard but the call of birds hemmed in by the ancient
      forest,

Male birds smoothly wheeling, following the females;

And there come to us the melancholy voices of the cuckoos

Out on the empty mountain, under the lonely moon . . .

Such travelling is harder than scaling the blue sky.

Even to hear of it turns the cheek pale,

With the highest crag barely a foot below heaven.

Dry pines hang, head down, from the face of the cliffs,

And a thousand plunging cataracts outroar one another

And send through ten thousand valleys a thunder of spinning
stones.

With all this danger upon danger,

Why do people come here who live at a safe distance?

. . . Though Dagger-Tower Pass be firm and grim,

And while one man guards it

Ten thousand cannot force it,

What if he be not loyal,

But a wolf toward his fellows?

. . . There are ravenous tigers to fear in the day

And venomous reptiles in the night

With their teeth and their fangs ready

To cut people down like hemp.

. . . Though the City of Silk be delectable, I would rather turn
home quickly.

Such travelling is harder than scaling the blue sky . . .

But I still face westward with a dreary moan.

(36)

ENDLESS YEARNING
(*Written to Music*)

I

" I am endlessly yearning
To be in Ch'ang-an.
. . . Insects hum of autumn by the gold brim of the well;
A thin frost glistens like little mirrors on my cold mat;
The high lantern flickers; and deeper grows my longing.
I lift the shade and, with many a sigh, gaze upon the moon,
Single as a flower, centred from the clouds.
Above, I see the blueness and deepness of sky.
Below, I see the greenness and the restlessness of water . . .
Heaven is high, earth wide; bitter between them flies my sorrow.
Can I dream through the gateway, over the mountain?
Endless longing
Breaks my heart."

II

" The sun has set, and a mist is in the flowers;
And the moon grows very white and people sad and sleepless.
A Chao harp has just been laid mute on its phœnix-holder,
And a Shu lute begins to sound its mandarin-duck strings . . .
Since nobody can bear to you the burden of my song,
Would that it might follow the spring wind to Yen-jan Mountain.
I think of you far away, beyond the blue sky,

And my eyes that once were sparkling
Are now a well of tears.
. . . Oh, if ever you should doubt this aching of my heart,
Here in my bright mirror come back and look at me! "

(37)

THE HARD ROAD

(*Written to Music*)

Pure wine costs, for the golden cup, ten thousand coppers a flagon,
And a jade plate of dainty food calls for a million coins.
I fling aside my food-sticks and cup, I cannot eat nor drink . . .
I pull out my dagger, I peer four ways in vain.
I would cross the Yellow River, but ice chokes the ferry;
I would climb the T'ai-hang Mountains, but the sky is blind with
    snow . . .
I would sit and poise a fishing-pole, lazy by a brook —
But I suddenly dream of riding a boat, sailing for the sun . . .
Journeying is hard,
Journeying is hard.
There are many turnings —
Which am I to follow? . . .
I will mount a long wind some day and break the heavy waves
And set my cloudy sail straight and bridge the deep, deep sea.

BRINGING IN THE WINE

(*Written to Music*)

See how the Yellow River's waters move out of heaven.
Entering the ocean, never to return.
See how lovely locks in bright mirrors in high chambers,
Though silken-black at morning, have changed by night to snow.
. . . Oh, let a man of spirit venture where he pleases
And never tip his golden cup empty toward the moon!
Since heaven gave the talent, let it be employed!
Spin a thousand pieces of silver, all of them come back!
Cook a sheep, kill a cow, whet the appetite,
And make me, of three hundred bowls, one long drink!
. . . To the old master, Ts'ên,
And the young scholar, Tan-ch'iu,
Bring in the wine!
Let your cups never rest!
Let me sing you a song!
Let your ears attend!
What are bell and drum, rare dishes and treasure?
Let me be forever drunk and never come to reason!
Sober men of olden days and sages are forgotten,
And only the great drinkers are famous for all time.
. . . Prince Ch'ên paid at a banquet in the Palace of Perfection
Ten thousand coins for a cask of wine, with many a laugh and
quip.
Why say, my host, that your money is gone?

Go and buy wine and we'll drink it together!
My flower-dappled horse,
My furs worth a thousand,
Hand them to the boy to exchange for good wine,
And we'll drown away the woes of ten thousand generations!

(38)

Li Shang-yin

隱商李

THE LO-YU TOMBS

With twilight shadows in my heart
I have driven up among the Lo-yu Tombs
To see the sun, for all his glory,
Buried by the coming night.

A NOTE ON A RAINY NIGHT
TO A FRIEND IN THE NORTH

You ask me when I am coming. I do not know.
I dream of your mountains and autumn pools brimming all night
with the rain.
Oh, when shall we be trimming wicks again, together in your
western window?
When shall I be hearing your voice again, all night in the rain?

A MESSAGE TO SECRETARY LING-HU

I am far from the clouds of Sung Mountain, a long way
    from trees in Ch'in;
And I send to you a message carried by two carp:
— Absent this autumn from the Prince's garden,
There's a poet at Mao-ling sick in the rain.

(39, 39a)

.

THERE IS ONLY ONE

There is only one Carved-Cloud, exquisite always —
Yet she dreads the spring, blowing cold in the palace,
When her husband, a Knight of the Golden Tortoise,
Will leave her sweet bed, to be early at court.

(40)

THE SUÊI PALACE

When gaily the Emperor toured the south
Contrary to every warning,
His whole empire cut brocades,
Half for wheel-guards, half for sails.

(4a)

THE JADE POOL

The Mother of Heaven, in her window by the Jade Pool,
Hears *The Yellow Bamboo Song* shaking the whole earth . . .
Where is Emperor Mu, with his eight horses running
Ten thousand miles a day? Why has he never come back?

(41)

TO THE MOON GODDESS

Now that a candle-shadow stands on the screen of carven marble
And the River of Heaven slants and the morning stars are low,
Are you sorry for having stolen the potion that has set you
Over purple seas and blue skies, to brood through the long
    nights?

(42, 4b)

CHIA YI

When the Emperor sought guidance from wise men, from exiles,
He found no calmer wisdom than that of young Chia
And assigned him the foremost council-seat at midnight,
Yet asked him about gods, instead of about people.

(43)

A CICADA

Pure of heart and therefore hungry,
All night long you have sung in vain —
Oh, this final broken indrawn breath
Among the green indifferent trees!
Yes, I have gone like a piece of driftwood,
I have let my garden fill with weeds. . . .
I bless you for your true advice
To live as pure a life as yours.

(44)

WIND AND RAIN

I ponder on the poem of *The Precious Dagger.*
My road has wound through many years.
. . . Now yellow leaves are shaken with a gale;
Yet piping and fiddling keep the Blue Houses merry.
On the surface, I seem to be glad of new people;
But doomed to leave old friends behind me,
I cry out from my heart for Shin-fêng wine
To melt away my thousand woes.

(45, 45ª)

FALLING PETALS

Gone is the guest from the Chamber of Rank,
And petals, confused in my little garden,
Zigzagging down my crooked path,
Escort like dancers the setting sun.
Oh, how can I bear to sweep them away?
To a sad-eyed watcher they never return.
Heart's fragrance is spent with the ending of spring
And nothing left but a tear-stained robe.

THOUGHTS IN THE COLD

You are gone. The river is high at my door.
Cicadas are mute on dew-laden boughs.
This is a moment when thoughts enter deep.
I stand alone for a long while.
. . . The North Star is nearer to me now than spring,
And couriers from your southland never arrive —
Yet I doubt my dream on the far horizon
That you have found another friend.

NORTH AMONG GREEN VINES

Where the sun has entered the western hills,
I look for a monk in his little straw hut;
But only the fallen leaves are at home,
And I turn through chilling levels of cloud.
I hear a stone gong in the dusk,
I lean full-weight on my slender staff . . .
How within this world, within this grain of dust,
Can there be any room for the passions of men?

THE INLAID HARP

I wonder why my inlaid harp has fifty strings,
Each with its flower-like fret an interval of youth.
. . . The sage Chuang-tzŭ is day-dreaming, bewitched by but-
terflies,
The spring-heart of Emperor Wang is crying in a cuckoo,
Mermen weep their pearly tears down a moon-green sea,
Blue fields are breathing their jade to the sun . . .
And a moment that ought to have lasted for ever
Has come and gone before I knew.

(46, 1a)

TO ONE UNNAMED

The stars of last night and the wind of last night
Are west of the Painted Chamber and east of Cinnamon Hall.
. . . Though I have for my body no wings like those of the bright-
coloured phœnix,
Yet I feel the harmonious heart-beat of the Sacred Unicorn.
Across the spring-wine, while it warms me, I prompt you how
to bet
Where, group by group, we are throwing dice in the light of a
crimson lamp;
Till the rolling of a drum, alas, calls me to my duties
And I mount my horse and ride away, like a water-plant cut
adrift.

(47)

THE PALACE OF THE SUÊI EMPEROR

His Palace of Purple Spring has been taken by mist and cloud,
As he would have taken all Yang-chou to be his private do-
main.
But for the seal of imperial jade being seized by the first T'ang
Emperor,
He would have bounded with his silken sails the limits of the
world.
Fire-flies are gone now, have left the weathered grasses,
But still among the weeping-willows crows perch at twilight.

. . . If he meets, there underground, the Later Ch'ên Emperor,
Do you think that they will mention *A Song of Courtyard
Flowers?*

(4a)

TO ONE UNNAMED

I

You said you would come, but you did not, and you left me with
no other trace
Than the moonlight on your tower at the fifth-watch bell.
I cry for you forever gone, I cannot waken yet,
I try to read your hurried note, I find the ink too pale.
. . . Blue burns your candle in its kingfisher-feather lantern
And a sweet breath steals from your hibiscus-broidered curtain.
But far beyond my reach is the Enchanted Mountain,
And you are on the other side, ten thousand peaks away.

II

A misty rain comes blowing with a wind from the east,
And wheels faintly thunder beyond Hibiscus Pool.
. . . Round the golden-toad lock, incense is creeping;
The jade tiger tells, on its cord, of water being drawn. . . .
A great lady once, from behind a screen, favoured a poor youth;
A fairy queen brought a bridal mat once for the ease of a prince
and then vanished.
. . . Must human hearts blossom in spring, like all other flowers?
And of even this bright flame of love, shall there be only ashes?

(48)

IN THE CAMP OF THE SKETCHING BRUSH

Monkeys and birds are still alert for your orders
And winds and clouds eager to shield your fortress.
. . . You were master of the brush, and a sagacious general,
But your Emperor, defeated, rode the prison-cart.
You were abler than even the greatest Chou statesmen,
Yet less fortunate than the two Shu generals who were killed in
    action.
And, though at your birth-place a temple has been built to you,
You never finished singing your *Song of the Holy Mountain.*

(49, 49c, 50)

TO ONE UNNAMED

Time was long before I met her, but is longer since we parted,
And the east wind has arisen and a hundred flowers are gone;
And the silk-worms of spring will weave until they die
And every night the candles will weep their wicks away.
Mornings in her mirror she sees her hair-cloud changing,
Yet she dares the chill of moonlight with her evening song.
. . . It is not so very far to her Enchanted Mountain —
O blue-birds, be listening! — Bring me what she says!

(39a)

SPRING RAIN

I am lying in a white-lined coat while the spring approaches,
But am thinking only of the White Gate City where I cannot be.
. . . There are two red chambers fronting the cold, hidden by the
    rain,
And a lantern on a pearl screen swaying my lone heart homeward.
. . . The long road ahead will be full of new hardship,
With, late in the nights, brief intervals of dream.
Oh, to send you this message, this pair of jade ear-rings! —
I watch a lonely wildgoose in three thousand miles of cloud.

(39a)

TO ONE UNNAMED

I

A faint phœnix-tail gauze, fragrant and doubled,
Lines your green canopy, closed for the night. . . .
Will your shy face peer round a moon-shaped fan,
And your voice be heard hushing the rattle of my carriage?
It is quiet and quiet where your gold lamp dies,
How far can a pomegranate-blossom whisper?
. . . I will tether my horse to a river willow
And wait for the will of the southwest wind.

II

There are many curtains in your care-free house,
Where rapture lasts the whole night long.
. . . What are the lives of angels but dreams
If they take no lovers into their rooms?
. . . Storms are ravishing the nut-horns,
Moon-dew sweetening cinnamon-leaves —
I know well enough naught can come of this union,
Yet how it serves to ease my heart!

THE HAN MONUMENT

The Son of Heaven in Yüan-ho times was martial as a god
And might be likened only to the Emperors Hsüan and Hsi.
He took an oath to reassert the glory of the empire,
And tribute was brought to his palace from all four quarters.
Western Huai for fifty years had been a bandit country,
Wolves becoming lynxes, lynxes becoming bears.
They assailed the mountains and rivers, rising from the plains,
With their long spears and sharp lances aimed at the Sun.
But the Emperor had a wise premier, by the name of Tu,
Who, guarded by spirits against assassination,
Hung at his girdle the seal of state, and accepted chief command,
While these savage winds were harrying the flags of the Ruler
    of Heaven.
Generals Suo, Wu, Ku, and T'ung became his paws and claws;

Civil and military experts brought their writing-brushes,

And his recording adviser was wise and resolute.

A hundred and forty thousand soldiers, fighting like lions and tigers,

Captured the bandit chieftains for the Imperial Temple.

So complete a victory was a supreme event;

And the Emperor said: "To you, Tu, should go the highest honour,

And your secretary, Yü, should write a record of it."

When Yü had bowed his head, he leapt and danced, saying:

"Historical writings on stone and metal are my especial art;

And, since I know the finest brush-work of the old masters,

My duty in this instance is more than merely official,

And I should be at fault if I modestly declined."

The Emperor, on hearing this, nodded many times.

And Yü retired and fasted and, in a narrow work-room,

His great brush thick with ink as with drops of rain,

Chose characters like those in the *Canons of Yao and Hsun*,

And a style as in the ancient poems *Ch'ing-miao* and *Shêng-min*.

And soon the description was ready, on a sheet of paper.

In the morning he laid it, with a bow, on the purple stairs.

He memorialized the throne: "I, unworthy,

Have dared to record this exploit, for a monument."

The tablet was thirty feet high, the characters large as dippers;

It was set on a sacred tortoise, its columns flanked with dragons . . .

The phrases were strange with deep words that few could understand;

And jealousy entered and malice and reached the Emperor —

So that a rope a hundred feet long pulled the tablet down
And coarse sand and small stones ground away its face.
But literature endures, like the universal spirit,
And its breath becomes a part of the vitals of all men.
The T'ang plate, the Confucian tripod, are eternal things,
Not because of their forms, but because of their inscriptions. . . .
Sagacious is our sovereign and wise his minister,
And high their successes and prosperous their reign;
But unless it be recorded by a writing such as this,
How may they hope to rival the three and five good rulers?
I wish I could write ten thousand copies to read ten thousand
    times,
Till spittle ran from my lips and calluses hardened my fingers,
And still could hand them down, through seventy-two generations,
As corner-stones for Rooms of Great Deeds on the Sacred Moun-
    tains.

(13, 51, 6)

Li Tüan

端 李

ON HEARING HER PLAY THE HARP

Her hands of white jade by a window of snow
Are glimmering on a golden-fretted harp—
And to draw the quick eye of Chou Yü,
She touches a wrong note now and then.

(52)

Li Yi

益 李

A SONG OF THE SOUTHERN RIVER
(*Written to Music*)

Since I married the merchant of Ch'ü-t'ang
He has failed each day to keep his word. . . .
Had I thought how regular the tide is,
I might rather have chosen a river-boy.

ON HEARING A FLUTE AT NIGHT
FROM THE WALL OF SHOU-HSIANG

The sand below the border-mountain lies like snow,
And the moon like frost beyond the city-wall,
And someone somewhere, playing a flute,
Has made the soldiers homesick all night long.

A BRIEF BUT HAPPY MEETING
WITH MY BROTHER-IN-LAW
"MEETING BY ACCIDENT, ONLY TO PART"

After these ten torn wearisome years
We have met again. We were both so changed
That hearing first your surname, I thought you a stranger —
Then hearing your given name, I remembered your young
    face. . . .
All that has happened with the tides
We have told and told till the evening bell. . . .
Tomorrow you journey to Yo-chou,
Leaving autumn between us, peak after peak.

Liu Chang-ch'ing
卿長劉

ON PARTING WITH THE BUDDHIST PILGRIM LING-CH'Ê

From the temple, deep in its tender bamboos,
Comes the low sound of an evening bell,
While the hat of a pilgrim carries the sunset
Farther and farther down the green mountain.

ON HEARING A LUTE-PLAYER

Your seven strings are like the voice
Of a cold wind in the pines,
Singing old beloved songs
Which no one cares for any more.

A FAREWELL TO A BUDDHIST MONK

Can drifting clouds and white storks
Be tenants in this world of ours? —
Or you still live on Wu-chou Mountain,
Now that people are coming here?

CLIMBING IN AUTUMN
FOR A VIEW FROM THE TEMPLE
ON THE TERRACE OF GENERAL WU

As the seasons have dealt with this ancient terrace,
So autumn breaks my homesick heart. . . .
Few pilgrims venture climbing to a temple so wild,
Up from the lake, in the mountain clouds.
. . . Sunset clings in the old defences,
A stone gong shivers through the empty woods.
. . . Of the Southern Dynasty, what remains?
Nothing but the great River.

(53)

A FAREWELL TO GOVERNOR LI
ON HIS WAY HOME TO HAN-YANG

Sad wanderer, once you conquered the South,
Commanding a hundred thousand men;
Today, dismissed and dispossessed,
In your old age you remember glory.
Once, when you stood, three borders were still;
Your dagger was the scale of life.
Now, watching the great rivers, the Kiang and the Han,
On their ways in the evening, where do you go?

ON SEEING WANG LEAVE FOR THE SOUTH

Toward a mist upon the water
Still I wave my hand and sob,
For the flying bird is lost in space
Beyond a desolate green mountain . . .
But now the long river, the far lone sail,
The five lakes, gleam like spring in the sunset;
And down an island white with duckweed
Comes the quiet of communion.

WHILE VISITING ON THE SOUTH STREAM
THE TAOIST PRIEST CH'ANG

Walking along a little path,
I find a footprint on the moss,
A white cloud low on the quiet lake,
Grasses that sweeten an idle door,
A pine grown greener with the rain,
A brook that comes from a mountain source —
And, mingling with Truth among the flowers,
I have forgotten what to say.

(75, 75a)

NEW YEAR'S AT CH'ANG-SHA

New Year's only deepens my longing,
Adds to the lonely tears of an exile
Who, growing old and still in harness,
Is left here by the homing spring . . .
Monkeys come down from the mountains to haunt me.
I bend like a willow, when it rains on the river.
I think of Chia Yi, who taught here and died here —
And I wonder what my term shall be.

(43)

ON LEAVING KIU-KIANG AGAIN
To Hsuëh and Liu

Dare I, at my age, accept my summons,
Knowing of the world's ways only wine and song? . . .
Over the moon-edged river come wildgeese from the Tartars;
And the thinner the leaves along the Huai, the wider the southern
    mountains . . .
I ought to be glad to take my old bones back to the capital,
But what am I good for in that world, with my few white
    hairs? . . .
As bent and decrepit as you are, I am ashamed to thank you,
When you caution me that I may encounter thunderbolts.

(54)

ON PASSING CHIA YI'S HOUSE IN CH'ANG-SHA

Here, where you spent your three years' exile,
To be mourned in Ch'u ten thousand years,
Can I trace your footprint in the autumn grass —
Or only slanting sunlight through the bleak woods?
If even good Emperor Wên was cold-hearted,
Could you hope that the dull river Hsiang would understand you,
These desolate waters, these taciturn mountains,
When you came, like me, so far away?

(43)

AN EVENING VIEW OF THE CITY OF YO-CHOU
AFTER COMING FROM HAN-KOU TO
PARROT ISLAND
A Poem Sent to My Friend Governor Yüan

No ripples in the river, no mist on the islands,
Yet the landscape is blurred toward my friend in Ch'u . . .
Birds in the slanting sun cross Han-kou,
And the autumn sky mingles with Lake Tung-t'ing.
. . . From a bleak mountain wall the cold tone of a bugle
Reminds me, moored by a ruined fort,
That Chia Yi's loyal plea to the House of Han
Banned him to Ch'ang-sha, to be an exile.

(43)

Liu Chung-yung
庸中柳

A TROOPER'S BURDEN

For years, to guard the Jade Pass and the River of Gold,
With our hands on our horse-whips and our sword-hilts,
We have watched the green graves change to snow
And the Yellow Stream ring the Black Mountain forever.

Liu Fang-p'ing
平方劉

A MOONLIGHT NIGHT

When the moon has coloured half the house,
With the North Star at its height and the South Star setting,
I can feel the first motions of the warm air of spring
In the singing of an insect at my green-silk window.

SPRING HEART-BREAK

With twilight passing her silken window,
She weeps alone in her chamber of gold;
For spring is departing from a desolate garden,
And a drift of pear-petals is closing a door.

Liu Shên-hsü

劉 眘 虛

A POEM

(Its Title Lost)

On a road outreaching the white clouds,
By a spring outrunning the bluest river,
Petals come drifting on the wind
And the brook is sweet with them all the way.
My quiet gate is a mountain-trail,
And the willow-trees about my cottage
Sift on my sleeve, through the shadowy noon,
Distillations of the sun.

Liu Tsung-yüan
元宗柳

RIVER-SNOW

A hundred mountains and no bird,
A thousand paths without a footprint;
A little boat, a bamboo cloak,
An old man fishing in the cold river-snow.

FROM THE CITY-TOWER OF LIU-CHOU
To My Four Fellow-Officials
at Chang, Ting, Fêng, and Lien Districts

At this lofty tower where the town ends, wilderness begins;
And our longing has as far to go as the ocean or the sky . . .
Hibiscus-flowers by the moat heave in a sudden wind,
And vines along the wall are whipped with slanting rain.
Nothing to see for three hundred miles but a blur of woods and
    mountain —
And the river's nine loops, twisting in our bowels. . . .
This is where they have sent us, this land of tattooed people —
And not even letters, to keep us in touch with home.

(55)

READING BUDDHIST CLASSICS WITH CH'AO
AT HIS TEMPLE IN THE EARLY MORNING

I clean my teeth in water drawn from a cold well;
And while I brush my clothes, I purify my mind;
Then, slowly turning pages in the Tree-Leaf Book,
I recite, along the path to the eastern shelter.
. . . The world has forgotten the true fountain of this teaching
And people enslave themselves to miracles and fables.
Under the given words I want the essential meaning,
I look for the simplest way to sow and reap my nature.
Here in the quiet of the priest's temple-courtyard,
Mosses add their climbing colour to the thick bamboo;
And now comes the sun, out of mist and fog,
And pines that seem to be new-bathed;
And everything is gone from me, speech goes, and reading,
Leaving the single unison.

DWELLING BY A STREAM

I had so long been troubled by official hat and robe
That I am glad to be an exile here in this wild southland.
I am a neighbour now of planters and reapers.
I am a guest of the mountains and woods.
I plough in the morning, turning dewy grasses,

And at evening tie my fisher-boat, breaking the quiet stream.
Back and forth I go, scarcely meeting anyone,
And sing a long poem and gaze at the blue sky.

AN OLD FISHERMAN

An old fisherman spent the night here, under the western cliff;
He dipped up water from the pure Hsiang and made a bamboo
fire;
And then, at sunrise, he went his way through the cloven mist,
With only the creak of his paddle left, in the greenness of moun-
tain and river.
. . . I turn and see the waves moving as from heaven,
And clouds above the cliffs coming idly, one by one.

Liu Yü-hsi

錫禹劉

BLACKTAIL ROW

Grass has run wild now by the Bridge of Red-Birds;
And swallows' wings, at sunset, in Blacktail Row
Where once they visited great homes,
Dip among doorways of the poor.

(56)

A SPRING SONG

In gala robes she comes down from her chamber
Into her courtyard, enclosure of spring . . .
When she tries from the centre to count the flowers,
On her hairpin of jade a dragon-fly poises.

IN THE TEMPLE OF THE FIRST KING OF SHU

Even in this world the spirit of a hero
Lives and reigns for thousands of years.

You were the firmest of the pot's three legs;
It was you who maintained the honour of the currency;
You chose a great premier to magnify your kingdom . . .
And yet you had a son so little like his father
That girls of your country were taken captive
To dance in the palace of the King of Wêi.

(49b, 49c)

THOUGHTS OF OLD TIME AT WEST FORT
MOUNTAIN

Since Wang Chün brought his towering ships down from Yi-chou,
The royal ghost has pined in the city of Nan-king.
Ten thousand feet of iron chain were sunk here to the bottom —
And then came the flag of surrender on the Wall of Stone. . . .
Cycles of change have moved into the past,
While still this mountain dignity has commanded the cold river;
And now comes the day of the Chinese world united,
And the old forts fill with ruin and with autumn reeds.

(57)

Lo Ping-wang

王賓駱

A POLITICAL PRISONER LISTENING TO A CICADA

While the year sinks westward, I hear a cicada
Bid me to be resolute here in my cell,
Yet it needed the song of those black wings
To break a white-haired prisoner's heart. . . .
His flight is heavy through the fog,
His pure voice drowns in the windy world.
Who knows if he be singing still? —
Who listens any more to me?

(58, 44)

Lu Lun

綸 盧

BORDER-SONGS

(*Written to Music*)

I

His golden arrow is tipped with hawk's feathers,
His embroidered silk flag has a tail like a swallow.
One man, arising, gives a new order
To the answering shout of a thousand tents.

II

The woods are black and a wind assails the grasses,
Yet the general tries night archery—
And next morning he finds his white-plumed arrow
Pointed deep in the hard rock.

III

High in the faint moonlight, wildgeese are soaring.
Tartar chieftains are fleeing through the dark—
And we chase them, with horses lightly burdened
And a burden of snow on our bows and our swords.

IV

Let feasting begin in the wild camp!
Let bugles cry our victory!
Let us drink, let us dance in our golden armour!
Let us thunder on rivers and hills with our drums!

(59)

A FAREWELL TO LI TUAN

By my old gate, among yellow grasses,
Still we linger, sick at heart.
The way you must follow through cold clouds
Will lead you this evening into snow.
Your father died; you left home young;
Nobody knew of your misfortunes.
We cry, we say nothing. What can I wish you,
In this blowing wintry world?

A NIGHT-MOORING AT WU-CHANG

Far off in the clouds stand the walls of Han-yang,
Another day's journey for my lone sail. . . .
Though a river-merchant ought to sleep in this calm weather,
I listen to the tide at night and voices of the boatmen.

. . . My thin hair grows wintry, like the triple Hsiang streams,
Three thousand miles my heart goes, homesick with the moon;
But the war has left me nothing of my heritage —
And oh, the pang of hearing these drums along the river!

Ma Tai
戴 馬

AN AUTUMN COTTAGE AT PA-SHANG

After the shower at Pa-shang,
I see an evening line of wildgeese,
The limp-hanging leaves of a foreign tree,
A lantern's cold gleam, lonely in the night,
An empty garden, white with dew,
The ruined wall of a neighbouring monastery.
. . . I have taken my ease here long enough.
What am I waiting for, I wonder.

THOUGHTS OF OLD TIME ON THE CH'U RIVER

A cold light shines on the gathering dew,
As sunset fades beyond the southern mountains;
Trees echo with monkeys on the banks of Lake Tung-t'ing,
Where somebody is moving in an orchid-wood boat.
Marsh-lands are swollen wide with the moon,
While torrents are bent to the mountains' will;
And the vanished Queens of the Clouds leave me
Sad with autumn all night long.

(60)

Mêng Chiao
郊 孟

A SONG OF A PURE-HEARTED GIRL
(*Written to Music*)

Lakka-trees ripen two by two
And mandarin-ducks die side by side.
If a true-hearted girl will love only her husband,
In a life as faithfully lived as theirs,
What troubling wave can arrive to vex
A spirit like water in a timeless well?

A TRAVELLER'S SONG
(*Written to Music*)

The thread in the hands of a fond-hearted mother
Makes clothes for the body of her wayward boy;
Carefully she sews and thoroughly she mends,
Dreading the delays that will keep him late from home.
But how much love has the inch-long grass
For three spring months of the light of the sun?

Mêng Hao-jan
然浩孟

A NIGHT-MOORING ON THE CHIEN-TÊ RIVER

While my little boat moves on its mooring of mist,
And daylight wanes, old memories begin. . . .
How wide the world was, how close the trees to heaven,
And how clear in the water the nearness of the moon!

A SPRING MORNING

I awake light-hearted this morning of spring,
Everywhere round me the singing of birds —
But now I remember the night, the storm,
And I wonder how many blossoms were broken.

A MESSAGE FROM LAKE TUNG-T'ING
TO PREMIER CHANG

Here in the Eighth-month the waters of the lake
Are of a single air with heaven,
And a mist from the Yun and Mêng valleys
Has beleaguered the city of Yo-chou.
I should like to cross, but I can find no boat.
. . . How ashamed I am to be idler than you statesmen,
As I sit here and watch a fisherman casting
And emptily envy him his catch.

ON CLIMBING YEN MOUNTAIN WITH FRIENDS

While worldly matters take their turn,
Ancient, modern, to and fro,
Rivers and mountains are changeless in their glory
And still to be witnessed from this trail.
. . . Where a fisher-boat dips by a waterfall,
Where the air grows colder, deep in the valley,
The monument of Yang remains;
And we have wept, reading the words.

(61)

AT A BANQUET
IN THE HOUSE OF THE TAOIST PRIEST MÊI

In my bed among the woods, grieving that spring must end,
I lifted up the curtain on a pathway of flowers,
And a flashing bluebird bade me come
To the dwelling-place of the Red Pine Genie.
. . . What a flame for his golden crucible —
Peach-trees magical with buds! —
And for holding boyhood in his face,
The rosy-flowing wine of clouds!

(62, 62a)

ON RETURNING AT THE YEAR'S END
TO CHUNG-NAN MOUNTAIN

I petition no more at the north palace-gate.
. . . To this tumble-down hut on Chung-nan Mountain
I was banished for my blunders, by a wise ruler.
I have been sick so long I see none of my friends.
My white hairs hasten my decline,
Like pale beams ending the old year.
Therefore I lie awake and ponder
On the pine-shadowed moonlight in my empty window.

(32, 32a)

STOPPING AT A FRIEND'S FARM-HOUSE

Preparing me chicken and rice, old friend,
You entertain me at your farm.
We watch the green trees that circle your village
And the pale blue of outlying mountains.
We open your window over garden and field,
To talk mulberry and hemp with our cups in our hands.
. . . Wait till the Mountain Holiday —
I am coming again in chrysanthemum time.

(64)

FROM CH'IN COUNTRY
TO THE BUDDHIST PRIEST YUAN

How gladly I would seek a mountain
If I had enough means to live as a recluse!
For I turn at last from serving the State
To the Eastern Woods Temple and to you, my master.
. . . Like ashes of gold in a cinnamon-flame,
My youthful desires have been burnt with the years —
And tonight in the chilling sunset-wind
A cicada, singing, weighs on my heart.

(63, 44)

FROM A MOORING ON THE T'UNG-LU TO A FRIEND IN YANG-CHOU

With monkeys whimpering on the shadowy mountain,
And the river rushing through the night,
And a wind in the leaves along both banks,
And the moon athwart my solitary sail,
I, a stranger in this inland district,
Homesick for my Yang-chou friends,
Send eastward two long streams of tears
To find the nearest touch of the sea.

TAKING LEAVE OF WANG WÊI

Slow and reluctant, I have waited
Day after day, till now I must go.
How sweet the road-side flowers might be
If they did not mean good-bye, old friend.
The Lords of the Realm are harsh to us
And men of affairs are not our kind.
I will turn back home, I will say no more,
I will close the gate of my old garden.

MEMORIES IN EARLY WINTER

South go the wildgeese, for leaves are now falling,
And the water is cold with a wind from the north.
I remember my home; but the Hsiang River's curves
Are walled by the clouds of this southern country.
I go forward. I weep till my tears are spent.
I see a sail in the far sky.
Where is the ferry? Will somebody tell me?
It's growing rough. It's growing dark.

ON CLIMBING ORCHID MOUNTAIN
IN THE AUTUMN
To Chang

On a northern peak among white clouds
You have found your hermitage of peace;
And now, as I climb this mountain to see you,
High with the wildgeese flies my heart.
The quiet dusk might seem a little sad
If this autumn weather were not so brisk and clear;
I look down at the river bank, with homeward-bound villagers
Resting on the sand till the ferry returns;
There are trees at the horizon like a row of grasses
And against the river's rim an island like the moon. . . .
I hope that you will come and meet me, bringing a basket of
   wine —
And we'll celebrate together the Mountain Holiday.

(64)

IN SUMMER AT THE SOUTH PAVILION
THINKING OF HSING

The mountain-light suddenly fails in the west,
In the east from the lake the slow moon rises.
I loosen my hair to enjoy the evening coolness
And open my window and lie down in peace.
The wind brings me odours of lotuses,
And bamboo-leaves drip with a music of dew. . . .
I would take up my lute and I would play,
But, alas, who here would understand?
And so I think of you, old friend,
O troubler of my midnight dreams!

AT THE MOUNTAIN-LODGE
OF THE BUDDHIST PRIEST YE
WAITING IN VAIN FOR MY FRIEND TING

Now that the sun has set beyond the western range,
Valley after valley is shadowy and dim . . .
And now through pine-trees come the moon and the chill of
    evening,
And my ears feel pure with the sound of wind and water. . . .
Nearly all the woodsmen have reached home,
Birds have settled on their perches in the quiet mist . . .

And still — because you promised — I am waiting for you, waiting,
Playing my lonely lute under a wayside vine.

RETURNING AT NIGHT TO LU-MÊN MOUNTAIN

A bell in the mountain-temple sounds the coming of night.
I hear people at the fishing-town stumble aboard the ferry,
While others follow the sand-bank to their homes along the river.
. . . I also take a boat and am bound for Lu-mên Mountain —
And soon the Lu-mên moonlight is piercing misty trees.
I have come, before I know it, upon an ancient hermitage,
The thatch door, the piney path, the solitude, the quiet,
Where a hermit lives and moves, never needing a companion.

(65)

One at the Western Front

人鄙西

GENERAL KÊ-SHU

This constellation, with its seven high stars,
Is Kê-shu lifting his sword in the night:
And no more barbarians, nor their horses, nor cattle,
Dare ford the river boundary.

(66)

P'ai Ti

迪 裴

A FAREWELL TO TS'UÊI

Though you think to return to this maze of mountains,
Oh, let them brim your heart with wonder! . . .
Remember the fisherman from Wu-ling
Who had only a day in the Peach-Blossom Country.

(2)

Po Chü-yi

易居白

A SUGGESTION TO MY FRIEND LIU

There's a gleam of green in an old bottle,
There's a stir of red in the quiet stove,
There's a feeling of snow in the dusk outside —
What about a cup of wine inside?

A SONG OF THE PALACE

Her tears are spent, but no dreams come.
She can hear the others singing through the night.
She has lost his love. Alone with her beauty,
She leans till dawn on her incense-pillow.

(67)

GRASSES

Boundless grasses over the plain
Come and go with every season;
Wildfire never quite consumes them —
They are tall once more in the spring wind.
Sweet they press on the old high-road
And reach the crumbling city-gate. . . .
O Prince of Friends, you are gone again. . . .
I hear them sighing after you.

(68)

TO MY BROTHERS AND SISTERS
ADRIFT IN TROUBLED TIMES
THIS POEM OF THE MOON

(*Since the disorders in Ho-nan and the famine in Kuan-nêi, my brothers and sisters have been scattered. Looking at the moon, I express my thoughts in this poem, which I send to my eldest brother at Fou-liang, my seventh brother at Yü-ch'ien, my fifteenth brother at Wu-chiang and my younger brothers and sisters at Fu-li and Hsia-kuêi.*)

My heritage lost through disorder and famine,
My brothers and sisters flung eastward and westward,
My fields and gardens wrecked by the war,

My own flesh and blood become scum of the street,
I moan to my shadow like a lone-wandering wildgoose,
I am torn from my root like a water-plant in autumn:
I gaze at the moon, and my tears run down
For hearts, in five places, all sick with one wish.

(69)

A SONG OF UNENDING SORROW

China's Emperor, craving beauty that might shake an empire,
Was on the throne for many years, searching, never finding,
Till a little child of the Yang clan, hardly even grown,
Bred in an inner chamber, with no one knowing her,
But with graces granted by heaven and not to be concealed,
At last one day was chosen for the imperial household.
If she but turned her head and smiled, there were cast a hundred
    spells,
And the powder and paint of the Six Palaces faded into nothing.
. . . It was early spring. They bathed her in the Flower-Pure Pool,
Which warmed and smoothed the creamy-tinted crystal of her skin,
And, because of her languor, a maid was lifting her
When first the Emperor noticed her and chose her for his bride.
The cloud of her hair, petal of her cheek, gold ripples of her crown
    when she moved,
Were sheltered on spring evenings by warm hibiscus-curtains;
But nights of spring were short and the sun arose too soon,
And the Emperor, from that time forth, forsook his early hearings

And lavished all his time on her with feasts and revelry,
His mistress of the spring, his despot of the night.
There were other ladies in his court, three thousand of rare beauty,
But his favours to three thousand were concentered in one body.
By the time she was dressed in her Golden Chamber, it would
    be almost evening;
And when tables were cleared in the Tower of Jade, she would
    loiter, slow with wine.
Her sisters and her brothers all were given titles;
And, because she so illumined and glorified her clan,
She brought to every father, every mother through the empire,
Happiness when a girl was born rather than a boy.
. . . High rose Li Palace, entering blue clouds,
And far and wide the breezes carried magical notes
Of soft song and slow dance, of string and bamboo music.
The Emperor's eyes could never gaze on her enough —
Till war-drums, booming from Yü-yang, shocked the whole earth
And broke the tunes of *The Rainbow Skirt and the Feathered
    Coat.*
The Forbidden City, the nine-tiered palace, loomed in the dust
From thousands of horses and chariots headed southwest.
The imperial flag opened the way, now moving and now
    pausing —
But thirty miles from the capital, beyond the western gate,
The men of the army stopped, not one of them would stir
Till under their horses' hoofs they might trample those moth-
    eyebrows . . .
Flowery hairpins fell to the ground, no one picked them up,
And a green and white jade hair-tassel and a yellow-gold hair-bird.

The Emperor could not save her, he could only cover his face.
And later when he turned to look, the place of blood and tears
Was hidden in a yellow dust blown by a cold wind.
. . . At the cleft of the Dagger-Tower Trail they criss-crossed
    through a cloud-line
Under O-mêi Mountain. The last few came.
Flags and banners lost their colour in the fading sunlight . . .
But as waters of Shu are always green and its mountains always
    blue,
So changeless was His Majesty's love and deeper than the days.
He stared at the desolate moon from his temporary palace.
He heard bell-notes in the evening rain, cutting at his breast.
And when heaven and earth resumed their round and the dragon-
    car faced home,
The Emperor clung to the spot and would not turn away
From the soil along the Ma-wêi slope, under which was buried
That memory, that anguish. Where was her jade-white face?
Ruler and lords, when eyes would meet, wept upon their coats
As they rode, with loose rein, slowly eastward, back to the capital.
. . . The pools, the gardens, the palace, all were just as before,
The Lake T'ai-yi hibiscus, the Wêi-yang Palace willows;
But a petal was like her face and a willow-leaf her eyebrow —
And what could he do but cry whenever he looked at them?
. . . Peach-trees and plum-trees blossomed, in the winds of spring;
Lakka-foliage fell to the ground, after autumn rains;
The Western and Southern Palaces were littered with late grasses,
And the steps were mounded with red leaves that no one swept
    away.
Her Pear-Garden Players became white-haired

And the eunuchs thin-eyebrowed in her Court of Pepper-Trees;
Over the throne flew fire-flies, while he brooded in the twilight.
He would lengthen the lamp-wick to its end and still could never
    sleep.
Bell and drum would slowly toll the dragging night-hours
And the River of Stars grow sharp in the sky, just before dawn,
And the porcelain mandarin-ducks on the roof grow thick with
    morning frost
And his covers of kingfisher-blue feel lonelier and colder
With the distance between life and death year after year;
And yet no beloved spirit ever visited his dreams.
. . . At Ling-ch'ün lived a Taoist priest who was a guest of
    heaven,
Able to summon spirits by his concentrated mind.
And people were so moved by the Emperor's constant brooding
That they besought the Taoist priest to see if he could find her.
He opened his way in space and clove the ether like lightning,
Up to heaven, under the earth, looking everywhere.
Above, he searched the Green Void, below, the Yellow Spring;
But he failed, in either place, to find the one he looked for.
And then he heard accounts of an enchanted isle at sea,
A part of the intangible and incorporeal world,
With pavilions and fine towers in the five-coloured air,
And of exquisite immortals moving to and fro,
And of one among them — whom they called The Ever True —
With a face of snow and flowers resembling hers he sought.
So he went to the West Hall's gate of gold and knocked at the
    jasper door
And asked a girl, called Morsel-of-Jade, to tell The Doubly-Perfect.

And the lady, at news of an envoy from the Emperor of China,
Was startled out of dreams in her nine-flowered canopy.
She pushed aside her pillow, dressed, shook away sleep,
And opened the pearly shade and then the silver screen.
Her cloudy hair-dress hung on one side because of her great haste,
And her flower-cap was loose when she came along the terrace,
While a light wind filled her cloak and fluttered with her motion
As though she danced *The Rainbow Skirt and the Feathered Coat.*
And the tear-drops drifting down her sad white face
Were like a rain in spring on the blossom of the pear.
But love glowed deep within her eyes when she bade him thank her liege,
Whose form and voice had been strange to her ever since their parting —
Since happiness had ended at the Court of the Bright Sun,
And moons and dawns had become long in Fairy-Mountain Palace.
But when she turned her face and looked down toward the earth
And tried to see the capital, there were only fog and dust.
So she took out, with emotion, the pledges he had given
And, through his envoy, sent him back a shell box and gold hairpin,
But kept one branch of the hairpin and one side of the box,
Breaking the gold of the hairpin, breaking the shell of the box;
"Our souls belong together," she said, "like this gold and this shell —
Somewhere, sometime, on earth or in heaven, we shall surely meet."

And she sent him, by his messenger, a sentence reminding him
Of vows which had been known only to their two hearts:
"On the seventh day of the Seventh-month, in the Palace of Long
    Life,
We told each other secretly in the quiet midnight world
That we wished to fly in heaven, two birds with the wings of one,
And to grow together on the earth, two branches of one tree."
. . . Earth endures, heaven endures; some time both shall end,
While this unending sorrow goes on and on for ever.

(4a, 4b, 70)

THE SONG OF A GUITAR

(*In the tenth year of Yuan-ho I was banished and demoted to
be assistant official in Kiu-kiang. In the summer of the next year
I was seeing a friend leave P'ên-p'u and heard in the midnight
from a neighbouring boat a guitar played in the manner of the
capital. Upon inquiry, I found that the player had formerly been a
dancing-girl there and in her maturity had been married to a mer-
chant. I invited her to my boat to have her play for us. She told
me her story, heyday and then unhappiness. Since, my departure
from the capital I had not felt sad; but that night, after I left her,
I began to realize my banishment. And I wrote this long poem —
six hundred and twelve characters.*)

I was bidding a guest farewell, at night on the Hsün-yang River,
Where maple-leaves and full-grown rushes rustled in the autumn.

I, the host, had dismounted, my guest had boarded his boat,

And we raised our cups and wished to drink — but, alas, there
  was no music.

For all we had drunk we felt no joy and were parting from each
  other,

When the river widened mysteriously toward the full moon —

We had heard a sudden sound, a guitar across the water.

Host forgot to turn back home, and guest to go his way.

We followed where the melody led and asked the player's name.

The sound broke off . . . then reluctantly she answered.

We moved our boat near hers, invited her to join us,

Summoned more wine and lanterns to recommence our banquet.

Yet we called and urged a thousand times before she started
  toward us,

Still hiding half her face from us behind her guitar.

. . . She turned the tuning-pegs and tested several strings;

We could feel what she was feeling, even before she played:

Each string a meditation, each note a deep thought,

As if she were telling us the ache of her whole life.

She knit her brows, flexed her fingers, then began her music,

Little by little letting her heart share everything with ours.

She brushed the strings, twisted them slow, swept them, plucked
  them —

First the air of *The Rainbow Skirt,* then *The Six Little Ones.*

The large strings hummed like rain,

The small strings whispered like a secret,

Hummed, whispered — and then were intermingled

Like a pouring of large and small pearls into a plate of jade.

We heard an oriole, liquid, hidden among flowers.

We heard a brook bitterly sob along a bank of sand. . . .
By the checking of its cold touch, the very string seemed broken
As though it could not pass; and the notes, dying away
Into a depth of sorrow and concealment of lament,
Told even more in silence than they had told in sound . . .
A silver vase abruptly broke with a gush of water,
And out leapt armoured horses and weapons that clashed and
　　smote —
And, before she laid her pick down, she ended with one stroke,
And all four strings made one sound, as of rending silk. . . .
There was quiet in the east boat and quiet in the west,
And we saw the white autumnal moon enter the river's heart.
. . . When she had slowly placed the pick back among the strings,
She rose and smoothed her clothing and, formal, courteous,
Told us how she had spent her girlhood at the capital,
Living in her parents' house under the Mount of Toads,
And had mastered the guitar at the age of thirteen,
With her name recorded first in the class-roll of musicians,
Her art the admiration even of experts,
Her beauty the envy of all the leading dancers,
How noble youths of Wu-ling had lavishly competed
And numberless red rolls of silk been given for one song,
And silver combs with shell inlay been snapped by her rhythms,
And skirts the colour of blood been spoiled with stains of wine . . .
Season after season, joy had followed joy,
Autumn moons and spring winds had passed without her heeding,
Till first her brother left for the war, and then her aunt died,
And evenings went and evenings came, and her beauty faded —
With ever fewer chariots and horses at her door;

So that finally she gave herself as wife to a merchant
Who, prizing money first, careless how he left her,
Had gone, a month before, to Fou-liang to buy tea.
And she had been tending an empty boat at the river's mouth,
No company but the bright moon and the cold water.
And sometimes in the deep of night she would dream of her
    triumphs
And be wakened from her dreams by the scalding of her tears.
. . . Her very first guitar-note had started me sighing;
Now, having heard her story, I was sadder still.
"We are both unhappy — to the sky's end.
We meet. We understand. What does acquaintance matter?
I came, a year ago, away from the capital
And am now a sick exile here in Kiu-kiang —
And so remote is Kiu-kiang that I have heard no music,
Neither string nor bamboo, for a whole year.
My quarters, near the River Town, are low and damp,
With bitter reeds and yellowed rushes all about the house.
And what is to be heard here, morning and evening? —
The bleeding cry of cuckoos, the whimpering of apes.
On flowery spring mornings and moonlit autumn nights
I have often taken wine up and drunk it all alone,
Of course there are the mountain songs and the village pipes,
But they are crude and strident, and grate on my ears.
And tonight, when I heard you playing your guitar,
I felt as if my hearing were bright with fairy-music.
Do not leave us. Come, sit down. Play for us again.
And I will write you a ballad to the tune you have just sung."
. . . Moved by what I said, she stood there for a moment,

Then sat again to her strings — and they sounded even sadder,
Although the tunes were different from those she had played
     before . . .
The feasters, all listening, covered their faces.
But who of them all was crying the most?
This Kiu-kiang official. My blue sleeve was wet.

(71)

Sêng Chiao-jan

然皎僧

NOT FINDING LU HUNG-CHIEN AT HOME

To find you, moved beyond the city,
A wide path led me, by mulberry and hemp,
To a new-set hedge of chrysanthemums —
Not yet blooming although autumn had come.
. . . I knocked; no answer, not even a dog.
I waited to ask your western neighbour;
But he told me that daily you climb the mountain,
Never returning until sunset.

(72)

Shên Ch'üan-ch'i
期 佺 沈

LINES

Against the City of the Yellow Dragon
Our troops were sent long years ago,
And girls here watch the same melancholy moon
That lights our Chinese warriors —
And young wives dream a dream of spring,
That last night their heroic husbands,
In a great attack, with flags and drums,
Captured the City of the Yellow Dragon.

BEYOND SEEING
(Written to Music)

A girl of the Lu clan who lives in Golden-Wood Hall,
Where swallows perch in pairs on beams of tortoise-shell,
Hears the washing-mallets' cold beat shake the leaves down.
. . . The Liao-yang expedition will be gone ten years,
And messages are lost in the White Wolf River.
. . . Here in the City of the Red Phœnix autumn nights are long,
Where one who is heart-sick to see beyond seeing,
Sees only moonlight on the yellow-silk wave of her loom.

(54)

Ssǔ-k'ung Shu

曙空司

A FAREWELL TO HAN SHEN
AT THE YUN-YANG INN

Long divided by river and sea,
For years we two have failed to meet —
And suddenly to find you seems like a dream. . . .
With a catch in the throat, we ask how old we are.
. . . Our single lamp shines, through cold and wet,
On a bamboo-thicket sheathed in rain;
But forgetting the sadness that will come with tomorrow,
Let us share the comfort of this farewell wine.

WHEN LU LUN MY COUSIN
COMES FOR THE NIGHT

With no other neighbour but the quiet night,
Here I live in the same old cottage;
And as raindrops brighten yellow leaves,
The lamp illumines my white head. . . .
Out of the world these many years,
I am ashamed to receive you here.
But you cannot come too often,
More than brother, lifelong friend.

TO A FRIEND BOUND NORTH
AFTER THE REBELLION

In dangerous times we two came south;
Now you go north in safety, without me.
But remember my head growing white among strangers,
When you look on the blue of the mountains of home.
. . . The moon goes down behind a ruined fort,
Leaving star-clusters above an old gate . . .
There are shivering birds and withering grasses,
Whichever way I turn my face.

Sung Chih-wên
問之宋

INSCRIBED ON THE WALL OF AN INN NORTH OF TA-YÜ MOUNTAIN

They say that wildgeese, flying southward,
Here turn back, this very month . . .
Shall my own southward journey
Ever be retraced, I wonder?
. . . The river is pausing at ebb-tide,
And the woods are thick with clinging mist —
But tomorrow morning, over the mountain,
Dawn will be white with the plum-trees of home.

(73)

Tai Shu-lun

倫叔戴

CHANCING ON OLD FRIENDS IN A VILLAGE INN

While the autumn moon is pouring full
On a thousand night-levels among towns and villages,
There meet by chance, south of the river,
Dreaming doubters of a dream . . .
In the trees a wind has startled the birds,
And insects cower from cold in the grass;
But wayfarers at least have wine
And nothing to fear — till the morning bell.

(74)

Ts'ên Ts'an

参 岑

ON MEETING A MESSENGER TO THE CAPITAL

It's a long way home, a long way east.
I am old and my sleeve is wet with tears.
We meet on horseback. I have no means of writing.
Tell them three words: " He is safe."

A MESSAGE TO CENSOR TU FU
AT HIS OFFICE IN THE LEFT COURT

Together we officials climbed vermilion steps,
To be parted by the purple walls . . .
Our procession, which entered the palace at dawn,
Leaves fragrant now at dusk with imperial incense.
. . . Grey heads may grieve for a fallen flower,
Or blue clouds envy a lilting bird;
But this reign is of heaven, nothing goes wrong,
There have been almost no petitions.

AN EARLY AUDIENCE AT THE PALACE OF LIGHT

HARMONIZING SECRETARY CHIA CHIH'S POEM

Cock-crow, the Purple Road cold in the dawn;
Linnet songs, court roofs tinted with April;
At the Golden Gate morning bell, countless doors open,
And up the jade steps float a thousand officials
With flowery scabbards. . . . Stars have gone down;
Willows are brushing the dew from the flags —
And, alone on the Lake of the Phœnix, a guest
Is chanting too well *The Song of Bright Spring.*

(9, 9a)

ASCENDING THE PAGODA
AT THE TEMPLE OF KIND FAVOUR

WITH KAO SHIH AND HSÜEH CH'Ü

The pagoda, rising abruptly from earth,
Reaches to the very Palace of Heaven . . .
Climbing, we seem to have left the world behind us,
With the steps we look down on hung from space.
It overtops a holy land
And can only have been built by toil of the spirit.
Its four sides darken the bright sun,
Its seven stories cut the grey clouds;
Birds fly down beyond our sight,

And the rapid wind below our hearing;
Mountain-ranges, toward the east,
Appear to be curving and flowing like rivers;
Far green locust-trees line broad roads
Toward clustered palaces and mansions;
Colours of autumn, out of the west,
Enter advancing through the city;
And northward there lie, in five graveyards,
Calm forever under dewy green grass,
Those who know life's final meaning
Which all humankind must learn.
. . . Henceforth I put my official hat aside.
To find the Eternal Way is the only happiness.

(75)

A SONG OF RUNNING-HORSE RIVER

In Farewell to General Fêng of the Western Expedition

Look how swift to the snowy sea races Running-Horse River!—
And sand, up from the desert, flies yellow into heaven.
This Ninth-month night is blowing cold at Wheel Tower,
And valleys, like peck measures, fill with the broken boulders
That downward, headlong, follow the wind.
. . . In spite of grey grasses, Tartar horses are plump;
West of the Hill of Gold, smoke and dust gather.
O General of the Chinese troops, start your campaign!
Keep your iron armour on all night long,

Send your soldiers forward with a clattering of weapons!
. . . While the sharp wind's point cuts the face like a knife,
And snowy sweat steams on the horses' backs,
Freezing a pattern of five-flower coins,
Your challenge from camp, from an inkstand of ice,
Has chilled the barbarian chieftain's heart.
You will have no more need of an actual battle! —
We await the news of victory, here at the western pass!

A SONG OF WHEEL TOWER

In Farewell to General Fêng of the Western Expedition

On Wheel Tower parapets night-bugles are blowing,
Though the flag at the northern end hangs limp.
Scouts, in the darkness, are passing Ch'ü-li,
Where, west of the Hill of Gold, the Tartar chieftain has
    halted. . . .
We can see, from the look-out, the dust and black smoke
Where Chinese troops are camping, north of Wheel Tower.
. . . Our flags now beckon the General farther west —
With bugles in the dawn he rouses his Grand Army;
Drums like a tempest pound on four sides
And the Yin Mountains shake with the shouts of ten thousand;
Clouds and the war-wind whirl up in a point
Over fields where grass-roots will tighten around white bones;
In the Dagger River mist, through a biting wind,
Horseshoes, at the Sand Mouth line, break on icy boulders.

. . . Our General endures every pain, every hardship,
Commanded to settle the dust along the border.
We have read, in the Green Books, tales of old days —
But here we behold a living man, mightier than the dead.

(76)

A SONG OF WHITE SNOW

IN FAREWELL TO FIELD-CLERK WU GOING HOME

The north wind rolls the white grasses and breaks them;
And the Eighth-month snow across the Tartar sky
Is like a spring gale, come up in the night,
Blowing open the petals of ten thousand pear-trees.
It enters the pearl blinds, it wets the silk curtains;
A fur coat feels cold, a cotton mat flimsy;
Bows become rigid, can hardly be drawn
And the metal of armour congeals on the men;
The sand-sea deepens with fathomless ice,
And darkness masses its endless clouds;
But we drink to our guest bound home from camp,
And play him barbarian lutes, guitars, harps;
Till at dusk, when the drifts are crushing our tents
And our frozen red flags cannot flutter in the wind,
We watch him through Wheel-Tower Gate going eastward
Into the snow-mounds of Heaven-Peak Road. . . .
And then he disappears at the turn of the pass,
Leaving behind him only hoof-prints.

Tsu Yung

詠 祖

ON SEEING THE SNOW-PEAK OF CHUNG-NAN

See how Chung-nan Mountain soars
With its white top over floating clouds —
And a warm sky opening at the snow-line
While the town in the valley grows colder and colder.

(32)

LOOKING TOWARD AN INNER GATE
OF THE GREAT WALL

My heart sank when I headed north from Yen Country
To the camps of China echoing with bugle and drum.
. . . In an endless cold light of massive snow,
Tall flags on three borders rise up like a dawn.
War-torches invade the barbarian moonlight,
Mountain-clouds like chairmen bear the Great Wall from the sea.
. . . Though no youthful clerk meant to be a great general, I
    throw aside my writing-brush —
Like the student who tossed off cap for a lariat, I challenge what
    may come.

(77)

Ts'uêi Hao
灝 崔

A SONG OF CH'ANG-KAN
(*Written to Music*)

I

"Tell me, where do you live? —
Near here, by the fishing-pool?
Let's hold our boats together, let's see
If we belong in the same town."

II

"Yes, I live here, by the river;
I have sailed on it many and many a time.
Both of us born in Ch'ang-kan, you and I!
Why haven't we always known each other?"

THE YELLOW CRANE TERRACE

Where long ago a yellow crane bore a sage to heaven,
Nothing is left now but the Yellow Crane Terrace.
The yellow crane never revisited earth,

And white clouds are flying without him for ever.
. . . Every tree in Han-yang becomes clear in the water,
And Parrot Island is a nest of sweet grasses;
But I look toward home, and twilight grows dark
With a mist of grief on the river waves.

(28a)

PASSING THROUGH HUA-YIN

Lords of the capital, sharp, unearthly,
The Great Flower's three points pierce through heaven.
Clouds are parting above the Temple of the Warring Emperor,
Rain dries on the mountain, on the Giant's Palm.
Ranges and rivers are the strength of this western gate,
Whence roads and trails lead downward into China.
. . . O pilgrim of fame, O seeker of profit,
Why not remain here and lengthen your days?

(14)

Ts'uĉi Shu

曙 崔

A CLIMB ON THE MOUNTAIN HOLIDAY
TO THE TERRACE WHENCE ONE SEES
THE MAGICIAN

A POEM SENT TO VICE-PREFECT LIU

The Han Emperor Wên bequeathed us this terrace
Which I climb to watch the coming dawn.
Cloudy peaks run northward in the three Chin districts,
And rains are blowing westward through the two Ling valleys.
. . . Who knows but me about the Guard at the Gate,
Or where the Magician of the River Bank is,
Or how to find that magistrate, that poet,
Who was as fond as I am of chrysanthemums and winecups?

(64, 43, 75a, 78, 2a)

Ts'uêi T'u

涂 崔

ON NEW YEAR'S EVE

Farther and farther from the three Pa Roads,
I have come three thousand miles, anxious and watchful,
Through pale snow-patches in the jagged night-mountains —
A stranger with a lonely lantern shaken in the wind.
. . . Separation from my kin
Binds me closer to my servants —
Yet how I dread, so far adrift,
New Year's Day, tomorrow morning!

A SOLITARY WILDGOOSE

Line after line has flown back over the border.
Where are you headed all by yourself?
In the evening rain you call to them —
And slowly you alight on an icy pond.
The low wet clouds move faster than you
Along the wall toward the cold moon.
. . . If they caught you in a net or with a shot,
Would it be worse than flying alone?

Tu Ch'iu-niang

娘秋杜

THE GOLD-THREADED ROBE

(*Written to Music*)

Covet not a gold-threaded robe,
Cherish only your young days!
If a bud open, gather it —
Lest you but wait for an empty bough.

(79)

Tu Fu

甫 杜

THE EIGHT-SIDED FORTRESS

The Three Kingdoms, divided, have been bound by his greatness.
The Eight-Sided Fortress is founded on his fame;
Beside the changing river, it stands stony as his grief
That he never conquered the Kingdom of Wu.

(49a, 52a)

ON MEETING LI KUÊI-NIEN DOWN THE RIVER

I met you often when you were visiting princes
And when you were playing in noblemen's halls.
. . . Spring passes. . . . Far down the river now,
I find you alone under falling petals.

(80, 4b)

ON A MOONLIGHT NIGHT

Far off in Fu-chou she is watching the moonlight,
Watching it alone from the window of her chamber —
For our boy and girl, poor little babes,
Are too young to know where the Capital is.
Her cloudy hair is sweet with mist,
Her jade-white shoulder is cold in the moon.
. . . When shall we lie again, with no more tears,
Watching this bright light on our screen?

A SPRING VIEW

Though a country be sundered, hills and rivers endure;
And spring comes green again to trees and grasses
Where petals have been shed like tears
And lonely birds have sung their grief.
. . . After the war-fires of three months,
One message from home is worth a ton of gold.
. . . I stroke my white hair. It has grown too thin
To hold the hairpins any more.

A NIGHT-VIGIL
IN THE LEFT COURT OF THE PALACE

Flowers are shadowed, the palace darkens,
Birds twitter by for a place to perch;
Heaven's ten thousand windows are twinkling,
And nine cloud-terraces are gleaming in the moonlight.
. . . While I wait for the golden lock to turn,
I hear jade pendants tinkling in the wind. . . .
I have a petition to present in the morning,
All night I ask what time it is.

TAKING LEAVE OF FRIENDS
ON MY WAY TO HUA-CHOU

*(In the second year of Chih-tê, I escaped from the capital through
the Gate of Golden Light and went to Fêng-hsiang. In the first
year of Ch'ien-yuan, I was appointed as official to Hua-chou
from my former post of Censor. Friends and relatives gathered and
saw me leave by the same gate. And I wrote this poem.)*

This is the road by which I fled,
When the rebels had reached the west end of the city;
And terror, ever since, has clutched at my vitals
Lest some of my soul should never return.
. . . The court has come back now, filling the capital;

But the Emperor sends me away again.
Useless and old, I rein in my horse
For one last look at the thousand gates.

(4d)

REMEMBERING MY BROTHERS
ON A MOONLIGHT NIGHT

A wanderer hears drums portending battle.
By the first call of autumn from a wildgoose at the border,
He knows that the dews tonight will be frost.
. . . How much brighter the moonlight is at home!
O my brothers, lost and scattered,
What is life to me without you?
Yet if missives in time of peace go wrong —
What can I hope for during war?

TO LI PO AT THE SKY'S END

A cold wind blows from the far sky. . . .
What are you thinking of, old friend?
The wildgeese never answer me.
Rivers and lakes are flooded with rain.
. . . A poet should beware of prosperity,
Yet demons can haunt a wanderer.
Ask an unhappy ghost, throw poems to him
Where he drowned himself in the Mi-lo River.

(81)

A FAREWELL AT FÊNG-CHI STATION
To General Yen

This is where your comrade must leave you,
Turning at the foot of these purple mountains. . . .
When shall we lift our cups again, I wonder,
As we did last night and walk in the moon?
The region is murmuring farewell
To one who was honoured through three reigns;
And back I go now to my river-village,
Into the final solitude.

ON LEAVING THE TOMB OF PREMIER FANG

Having to travel back now from this far place,
I dismount beside your lonely tomb.
The ground where I stand is wet with my tears;
The sky is dark with broken clouds. . . .
I who played chess with the great Premier
Am bringing to my lord the dagger he desired. . . .
But I find only petals falling down,
I hear only linnets answering.

(82)

A NIGHT ABROAD

A light wind is rippling at the grassy shore. . . .
Through the night, to my motionless tall mast,
The stars lean down from open space,
And the moon comes running up the river.
. . . If only my art might bring me fame
And free my sick old age from office! —
Flitting, flitting, what am I like
But a sand-snipe in the wide, wide world!

ON THE GATE-TOWER AT YO-CHOU

I had always heard of Lake Tung-t'ing —
And now at last I have climbed to this tower.
With Wu country to the east of me and Ch'u to the south,
I can see heaven and earth endlessly floating.
. . . But no word has reached me from kin or friends.
I am old and sick and alone with my boat.
North of this wall there are wars and mountains —
And here by the rail how can I help crying?

THE TEMPLE OF THE PREMIER OF SHU

Where is the temple of the famous Premier? —
In a deep pine grove near the City of Silk,
With the green grass of spring colouring the steps,
And birds chirping happily under the leaves.
. . . The third summons weighted him with affairs of state
And to two generations he gave his true heart,
But before he could conquer, he was dead;
And heroes have wept on their coats ever since.

(49b)

A HEARTY WELCOME
To Vice-Prefect Ts'uêi

North of me, south of me, spring is in flood,
Day after day I have seen only gulls . . .
My path is full of petals — I have swept it for no others.
My thatch gate has been closed — but opens now for you.
It's a long way to the market, I can offer you little —
Yet here in my cottage there is old wine for our cups.
Shall we summon my elderly neighbour to join us,
Call him through the fence, and pour the jar dry?

A VIEW OF THE WILDERNESS

Snow is white on the westward mountains and on three forti-
    fied towns,
And waters in this southern lake flash on a long bridge.
But wind and dust from sea to sea bar me from my brothers;
And I cannot help crying, I am so far away.
I have nothing to expect now but the ills of old age.
I am of less use to my country than a grain of dust.
I ride out to the edge of town. I watch on the horizon,
Day after day, the chaos of the world.

BOTH SIDES OF THE YELLOW RIVER
RECAPTURED BY THE IMPERIAL ARMY

News at this far western station! The north has been recaptured!
At first I cannot check the tears from pouring on my coat —
Where is my wife? Where are my sons?
Yet crazily sure of finding them, I pack my books and poems —
And loud my song and deep my drink
On the green spring-day that starts me home,
Back from this mountain, past another mountain,
Up from the south, north again — to my own town!

(83)

A LONG CLIMB

In a sharp gale from the wide sky apes are whimpering,
Birds are flying homeward over the clear lake and white sand,
Leaves are dropping down like the spray of a waterfall,
While I watch the long river always rolling on.
I have come three thousand miles away. Sad now with autumn
And with my hundred years of woe, I climb this height alone.
Ill fortune has laid a bitter frost on my temples,
Heart-ache and weariness are a thick dust in my wine.

FROM AN UPPER STORY

Flowers, as high as my window, hurt the heart of a wanderer
For I see, from this high vantage, sadness everywhere.
The Silken River, bright with spring, floats between earth and
    heaven
Like a line of cloud by the Jade Peak, between ancient days and
    now.
. . . Though the State is established for a while as firm as the
    North Star
And bandits dare not venture from the western hills,
Yet sorry in the twilight for the woes of a long-vanished Emperor,
I am singing the song his Premier sang when still unestranged
    from the mountain.

(49c)

STAYING AT THE GENERAL'S HEADQUARTERS

The autumn night is clear and cold in the lakka-trees of this
    courtyard.
I am lying forlorn in the river-town. I watch my guttering candle.
I hear the lonely notes of a bugle sounding through the dark.
The moon is in mid-heaven, but there's no one to share it with me.
My messengers are scattered by whirls of rain and sand.
City-gates are closed to a traveller; mountains are walls in my
    way —
Yet, I who have borne ten years of pitiable existence,
Find here a perch, a little branch, and am safe for this one night.

NIGHT IN THE WATCH-TOWER

While winter daylight shortens in the elemental scale
And snow and frost whiten the cold-circling night,
Stark sounds the fifth-watch with a challenge of drum and bugle.
. . . The stars and the River of Heaven pulse over the three moun-
    tains;
I hear women in the distance, wailing after the battle;
I see barbarian fishermen and woodcutters in the dawn.
. . . Sleeping-Dragon, Plunging-Horse, are no generals now, they
    are dust —
Hush for a moment, O tumult of the world.

(84, 49d)

THOUGHTS OF OLD TIME

I

Ten thousand ranges and valleys approach the Ching Gate
And the village in which the Lady of Light was born and bred.
She went out from the purple palace into the desert-land;
She has now become a green grave in the yellow dusk.
Her face! — Can you picture a wind of the spring?
Her spirit by moonlight returns with a tinkling
Song of the Tartars on her jade guitar,
Telling her eternal sorrow.

(25a)

II

Chu-kê's prestige transcends the earth;
There is only reverence for his face;
Yet his will, among the Three Kingdoms at war,
Was only as one feather against a flaming sky.
He was brother of men like Yi and Lü
And in time would have surpassed the greatest of all statesmen.
Though he knew there was no hope for the House of Han,
Yet he wielded his mind for it, yielded his life.

(49, 49b, 49c, 85)

A VIEW OF T'AI-SHAN

What shall I say of the Great Peak? —
The ancient dukedoms are everywhere green,
Inspired and stirred by the breath of creation,
With the Twin Forces balancing day and night.
. . . I bare my breast toward opening clouds,
I strain my sight after birds flying home.
When shall I reach the top and hold
All mountains in a single glance?

(14, 19)

TO MY RETIRED FRIEND WÊI

It is almost as hard for friends to meet
As for the morning and evening stars.
Tonight then is a rare event,
Joining, in the candlelight,
Two men who were young not long ago
But now are turning grey at the temples.
. . . To find that half our friends are dead
Shocks us, burns our hearts with grief.
We little guessed it would be twenty years
Before I could visit you again.
When I went away, you were still unmarried;
But now these boys and girls in a row

Are very kind to their father's old friend.
They ask me where I have been on my journey;
And then, when we have talked awhile,
They bring and show me wines and dishes,
Spring chives cut in the night-rain
And brown rice cooked freshly a special way.
. . . My host proclaims it a festival,
He urges me to drink ten cups —
But what ten cups could make me as drunk
As I always am with your love in my heart?
. . . Tomorrow the mountains will separate us;
After tomorrow — who can say?

ALONE IN HER BEAUTY

Who is lovelier than she?
Yet she lives alone in an empty valley.
She tells me she came from a good family
Which is humbled now into the dust.
. . . When trouble arose in the Kuan district,
Her brothers and close kin were killed.
What use were their high offices,
Not even shielding their own lives? —
The world has but scorn for adversity;
Hope goes out, like the light of a candle.
Her husband, with a vagrant heart,
Seeks a new face like a new piece of jade;
And when morning-glories furl at night

And mandarin-ducks lie side by side,
All he can see is the smile of the new love,
While the old love weeps unheard.
The brook was pure in its mountain source,
But away from the mountain its waters darken.
. . . Waiting for her maid to come from selling pearls
For straw to cover the roof again,
She picks a few flowers, no longer for her hair,
And lets pine-needles fall through her fingers,
And, forgetting her thin silk sleeve and the cold,
She leans in the sunset by a tall bamboo.

SEEING LI PO IN A DREAM

I

There are sobs when death is the cause of parting;
But life has its partings again and again.
. . . From the poisonous damps of the southern river
You had sent me not one sign from your exile —
Till you came to me last night in a dream,
Because I am always thinking of you. . . .
I wondered if it were really you,
Venturing so long a journey.
You came to me through the green of a forest,
You disappeared by a shadowy fortress . . .
Yet out of the midmost mesh of your snare,

How could you lift your wings and use them?
. . . I woke, and the low moon's glimmer on a rafter
Seemed to be your face, still floating in the air.
. . . There were waters to cross, they were wild and
     tossing;
If you fell, there were dragons and river-monsters.

II

This cloud, that has drifted all day through the sky,
May, like a wanderer, never come back. . . .
Three nights now I have dreamed of you —
As tender, intimate and real as though I were awake.
And then, abruptly rising to go,
You told me the perils of adventure
By river and lake — the storms, the wrecks,
The fears that are borne on a little boat;
And, here in my doorway, you rubbed your white head
As if there were something puzzling you.
. . . Our capital teems with officious people,
While you are alone and helpless and poor.
Who says that the heavenly net never fails?
It has brought you ill fortune, old as you are.
. . . A thousand years' fame, ten thousand years'
     fame —
What good, when you are dead and gone?

(86)

A DRAWING OF A HORSE BY GENERAL TS'AO
AT SECRETARY WÊI FÊNG'S HOUSE

Throughout this dynasty no one had painted horses
Like the master-spirit, Prince Chiang-tu —
And then to General Ts'ao through his thirty years of fame
The world's gaze turned, for royal steeds.
He painted the late Emperor's luminous white horse.
For ten days the thunder flew over Dragon Lake,
And a pink-agate plate was sent him from the palace —
The talk of the court-ladies, the marvel of all eyes.
The General danced, receiving it in his honoured home. . . .
After this rare gift, followed rapidly fine silks
From many of the nobles, requesting that his art
Lend a new lustre to their screens.
. . . First came the curly-maned horse of Emperor T'ai-tsung,
Then, for the Kuos, a lion-spotted horse . . .
But now in this painting I see two horses,
A sobering sight for whosoever knew them.
They are war-horses. Either could face ten thousand.
They make the white silk stretch away into a vast desert.
And the seven others with them are almost as noble. . . .
Mist and snow are moving across a cold sky,
And hoofs are cleaving snow-drifts under great trees —
With here a group of officers and there a group of servants.
See how these nine horses all vie with one another —
The high clear glance, the deep firm breath.
. . . Who understands distinction? Who really cares for art?

You, Wêi Fêng, have followed Ts'ao; Chih Tun preceded
   him.

. . . I remember when the late Emperor came toward his Summer
   Palace,

The procession, in green-feathered rows, swept from the east-
   ern sky —

Thirty thousand horses, prancing, galloping,

Fashioned, every one of them, like the horses in this picture. . . .

But now the Imperial Ghost receives secret jade from the River-
   God,

For the Emperor hunts crocodiles no longer by the streams.

Where you see his Great Gold Tomb, you may hear among the
   pines

A bird grieving in the wind that the Emperor's horses are gone.

(87)

A SONG OF A PAINTING
To General Ts'ao

   O General, descended from Wêi's Emperor Wu,
   You are nobler now than when a noble. . . .
   Conquerors and their valour perish,
   But masters of beauty live forever.
   . . . With your brush-work learned from Lady Wêi
   And second only to Wang Hsi-chih's,
   Faithful to your art, you know no age,
   Letting wealth and fame drift by like clouds.

. . . In the years of K'ai-yüan you were much with the Emperor,
Accompanied him often to the Court of the South Wind.
When the spirit left great statesmen, on walls of the Hall of
  Fame
The point of your brush preserved their living faces.
You crowned all the premiers with coronets of office;
You fitted all commanders with arrows at their girdles;
You made the founders of this dynasty, with every hair alive,
Seem to be just back from the fierceness of a battle.
. . . The late Emperor had a horse, known as Jade Flower,
Whom artists had copied in various poses.
They led him one day to the red marble stairs
With his eyes toward the palace in the deepening air.
Then, General, commanded to proceed with your work,
You centred all your being on a piece of silk.
And later, when your dragon-horse, born of the sky,
Had banished earthly horses for ten thousand generations,
There was one Jade Flower standing on the dais
And another by the steps, and they marvelled at each other. . . .
The Emperor rewarded you with smiles and with gifts,
While officers and men of the stud hung about and stared.
. . . Han Kan, your follower, has likewise grown proficient
At representing horses in all their attitudes;
But picturing the flesh, he fails to draw the bone —
So that even the finest are deprived of their spirit.
You, beyond the mere skill, used your art divinely —
And expressed, not only horses, but the life of a good man. . . .
Yet here you are, wandering in a world of disorder
And sketching from time to time some petty passer-by.

People note your case with the whites of their eyes.
There's nobody purer, there's nobody poorer.
. . . Read in the records, from earliest times,
How hard it is to be a great artist.

(88)

A LETTER TO CENSOR HAN

I am sad. My thoughts are in Yo-chou.
I would hurry there — but I am sick in bed.
. . . Beauty would be facing me across the autumn waters.
Oh, to wash my feet in Lake Tung-t'ing and see at its eight corners
Wildgeese flying high, sun and moon both white,
Green maples changing to red in the frosty sky,
Angels bound for the Capital of Heaven, near the North Star,
Riding, some of them phœnixes, and others unicorns,
With banners of hibiscus and with melodies of mist,
Their shadows dancing upside-down in the southern rivers,
Till the Queen of the Stars, drowsy with her nectar,
Would forget the winged men on either side of her!
. . . From the Wizard of the Red Pine this word has come for
    me:
That after his earlier follower he has now a new disciple
Who, formerly at the capital as Emperor Liu's adviser,
In spite of great successes, never could be happy.
. . . What are a country's rise and fall?
Can flesh-pots be as fragrant as mountain fruit? . . .

I grieve that he is lost far away in the south.
May the star of long life accord him its blessing!
. . . O purity, to seize you from beyond the autumn waters
And to place you as an offering in the Court of Imperial Jade.

(89)

A SONG OF AN OLD CYPRESS

Beside the Temple of the Great Premier stands an ancient cypress
With a trunk of green bronze and a root of stone.
The girth of its white bark would be the reach of forty men
And its tip of kingfisher-blue is two thousand feet in heaven.
Dating from the days of a great ruler's great statesman,
Their very tree is loved now and honoured by the people.
Clouds come to it from far away, from the Wu cliffs,
And the cold moon glistens on its peak of snow.
. . . East of the Silk Pavilion yesterday I found
The ancient ruler and wise statesman both worshipped in one
    temple,
Whose tree, with curious branches, ages the whole landscape
In spite of the fresh colours of the windows and the doors.
And so firm is the deep root, so established underground,
That its lone lofty boughs can dare the weight of winds,
Its only protection the Heavenly Power,
Its only endurance the art of its Creator.
. . . When beams are required to restore a great house,
Though oxen sway ten thousand heads, they cannot move a
    mountain.

Though a tree writes no memorial, yet people understand
That not unless they fell it can use be made of it. . . .
Its bitter heart may be tenanted now by black and white ants,
But its odorous leaves were once the nest of phœnixes and
    pheasants.
. . . Let wise and hopeful men harbour no complaint.
The greater the timber, the tougher it is to use.

(90)

A SONG OF DAGGER-DANCING
To a Girl-Pupil of Lady Kung-sun

*(On the 19th of the Tenth-month in the second year of Ta-li,
I saw, in the house of the K'uêi-fu official Yüan T'ê, a girl named
Li from Ling-ying dancing with a dagger. I admired her skill
and asked who was her teacher. She named Lady Kung-sun. I
remembered that in the third year of K'ai-yüan at Yen-ch'êng,
when I was a little boy, I saw Lady Kung-sun dance. She was the
only one in the Imperial Theatre who could dance with this
weapon. Now she is aged and unknown, and even her pupil has
passed the heyday of beauty. I wrote this poem to express my wist-
fulness. The work of Chang Hsü of the Wu district, that great
master of grassy writing, was improved by his having been present
when Lady Kung-sun danced in the Yieh district. From this may
be judged the art of Kung-sun.)*

There lived years ago the beautiful Kung-sun,
Who, dancing with her dagger, drew from all four quarters

An audience like mountains lost among themselves.

Heaven and earth moved back and forth, following her motions,

Which were bright as when the Archer shot the nine suns down
    the sky

And rapid as angels before the wings of dragons.

She began like a thunderbolt, venting its anger,

And ended like the shining calm of rivers and the sea . . .

But vanished are those red lips and those pearly sleeves;

And none but this one pupil bears the perfume of her fame,

This beauty from Ling-ying, at the Town of the White God,

Dancing still and singing in the old blithe way.

And while we reply to each other's questions,

We sigh together, saddened by changes that have come.

There were eight thousand ladies in the late Emperor's court,

But none could dance the dagger-dance like Lady Kung-sun.

. . . Fifty years have passed, like the turning of a palm;

Wind and dust, filling the world, obscure the Imperial House.

Instead of the Pear-Garden Players, who have blown by like a mist,

There are one or two girl-musicians now — trying to charm the
    cold Sun.

There are man-size trees by the Emperor's Golden Tomb. . . .

I seem to hear dead grasses rattling on the cliffs of Ch'ü-t'ang.

. . . The song is done, the slow string and quick pipe have
    ceased.

At the height of joy, sorrow comes with the eastern moon rising.

And I, a poor old man, not knowing where to go,

Must harden my feet on the lone hills, toward sickness and despair.

(91)

A SONG OF WAR-CHARIOTS

(Written to Music)

The war-chariots rattle,
The war-horses whinny.
Each man of you has a bow and a quiver at his belt.
Father, mother, son, wife, stare at you going,
Till dust shall have buried the bridge beyond Ch'ang-an.
They run with you, crying, they tug at your sleeves,
And the sound of their sorrow goes up to the clouds;
And every time a bystander asks you a question,
You can only say to him that you have to go.
. . . We remember others at fifteen sent north to guard the river
And at forty sent west to cultivate the camp-farms.
The mayor wound their turbans for them when they started out.
With their turbaned hair white now, they are still at the border,
At the border where the blood of men spills like the sea —
And still the heart of Emperor Wu is beating for war.
. . . Do you know that, east of China's mountains, in two hundred districts
And in thousands of villages, nothing grows but weeds,
And though strong women have bent to the ploughing,
East and west the furrows all are broken down?
. . . Men of China are able to face the stiffest battle,
But their officers drive them like chickens and dogs.
Whatever is asked of them,
Dare they complain?
For example, this winter

Held west of the gate,
Challenged for taxes,
How could they pay?
. . . We have learned that to have a son is bad luck —
It is very much better to have a daughter
Who can marry and live in the house of a neighbour,
While under the sod we bury our boys.
. . . Go to the Blue Sea, look along the shore
At all the old white bones forsaken —
New ghosts are wailing there now with the old,
Loudest in the dark sky of a stormy day.

A SONG OF FAIR WOMEN
(*Written to Music*)

On the third day of the Third-month in the freshening weather
Many beauties take the air by the Ch'ang-an water-front,
Receptive, aloof, sweet-mannered, sincere,
With soft fine skin and well-balanced bone.
Their embroidered silk robes in the spring sun are gleaming
With a mass of golden peacocks and silver unicorns.
And hanging far down from their temples
Are blue leaves of delicate kingfisher feathers.
And following behind them
Is a pearl-laden train, rhythmic with bearers.
Some of them are kindred to the Royal House —
The titled Princesses Kuo and Ch'in.

Red camel-humps are brought them from jade broilers,
And sweet fish is offered them on crystal trays.
Though their food-sticks of unicorn-horn are lifted languidly
And the finely wrought phœnix carving-knife is very little used,
Fleet horses from the Yellow Gate, stirring no dust,
Bring precious dishes constantly from the imperial kitchen.
. . . While a solemn sound of flutes and drums invokes gods
    and spirits,
Guests and courtiers gather, all of high rank;
And finally, riding slow, a dignified horseman
Dismounts at the pavilion on an embroidered rug.
In a snow of flying willow-cotton whitening the duckweed,
Bluebirds find their way with vermilion handkerchiefs —
But power can be as hot as flame and burn people's fingers.
Be wary of the Premier, watch for his frown.

(4)

A SONG OF SOBBING BY THE RIVER
(*Written to Music*)

I am only an old woodsman, whispering a sob,
As I steal like a spring-shadow down the Winding River.
. . . Since the palaces ashore are sealed by a thousand gates —
Fine willows, new rushes, for whom are you so green?
. . . I remember a cloud of flags that came from the South Garden,
And ten thousand colours, heightening one another,
And the Kingdom's first Lady, from the Palace of the Bright Sun,

Attendant on the Emperor in his royal chariot,
And the horsemen before them, each with bow and arrows,
And the snowy horses, champing at bits of yellow gold,
And an archer, breast skyward, shooting through the clouds
And felling with one dart a pair of flying birds.
. . . Where are those perfect eyes, where are those pearly teeth?
A blood-stained spirit has no home, has nowhere to return.
And clear Wêi waters running east, through the cleft on Dagger-
   Tower Trail,
Carry neither there nor here any news of her.
People, compassionate, are wishing with tears
That she were as eternal as the river and the flowers.
. . . Mounted Tartars, in the yellow twilight, cloud the town
   with dust.
I am fleeing south, but I linger — gazing northward toward the
   throne.

(4a)

A SONG OF A PRINCE DEPOSED
(*Written to Music*)

Along the wall of the Capital a white-headed crow
Flies to the Gate where Autumn Enters and screams there in the
   night,
Then turns again and pecks among the roofs of a tall mansion
Whose lord, a mighty mandarin, has fled before the Tartars,
With his golden whip now broken, his nine war-horses dead

And his own flesh and bone scattered to the winds. . . .
There's a rare ring of green coral underneath the vest
Of a Prince at a street-corner, bitterly sobbing,
Who has to give a false name to anyone who asks him —
Just a poor fellow, hoping for employment.
A hundred days' hiding in grasses and thorns
Show on his body from head to foot.
But, since their first Emperor, all with hook-noses,
These Dragons look different from ordinary men.
Wolves are in the palace now and Dragons are lost in the desert —
O Prince, be very careful of your most sacred person!
I dare not address you long, here by the open road,
Nor even to stand beside you for more than these few moments.
Last night with the spring-wind there came a smell of blood;
The old Capital is full of camels from the east.
Our northern warriors are sound enough of body and of hand —
Oh, why so brave in olden times and so craven now?
Our Emperor, we hear, has given his son the throne
And the southern border-chieftains are loyally inclined
And the Hua-mên and Li-mien tribes are gathering to avenge us.
But still be careful — keep yourself well hidden from the dagger.
Unhappy Prince, I beg you, be constantly on guard —
Till power blow to your aid from the Five Imperial Tombs.

(4d, 92)

Tu Hsün-hê

鶴 荀 杜

A SIGH IN THE SPRING PALACE

Knowing beauty my misfortune,
I face my mirror with a sigh.
To please a fastidious emperor,
How shall I array myself? . . .
Birds flock and sing when the wind is warm,
Flower-shadows climb when the sun is high —
And year after year girls in the south
Are picking hibiscus, dreaming of love!

(93)

Tu Mu
牧 杜

I CLIMB TO THE LO-YU TOMBS
BEFORE LEAVING FOR WU-HSING

Even in this good reign, how can I serve?
The lone cloud rather, the Buddhist peace . . .
Once more, before crossing river and sea,
I face the great Emperor's mountain-tomb.

(94)

BY THE PURPLE CLIFF

On a part of a spear still unrusted in the sand
I have burnished the symbol of an ancient kingdom. . . .
Except for a wind aiding General Chou Yü,
Spring would have sealed both Ch'iao girls in Copper-Bird Palace.

(52a)

A MOORING ON THE CH'IN-HUAI RIVER

Mist veils the cold stream, and moonlight the sand,
As I moor in the shadow of a river-tavern,
Where girls, with no thought of a perished kingdom,
Gaily echo *A Song of Courtyard Flowers*.

(4a)

A MESSAGE TO HAN CHO
THE YANG-CHOU MAGISTRATE

There are faint green mountains and far green waters,
And grasses in this river region not yet faded by autumn;
And clear in the moon on the Twenty-Four Bridges,
Girls white as jade are teaching flute-music.

(95)

A CONFESSION

With my wine-bottle, watching by river and lake
For a lady so tiny as to dance on my palm,
I awake, after dreaming ten years in Yang-chou,
Known as fickle, even in the Street of Blue Houses.

(26a, 45a)

IN THE AUTUMN NIGHT

Her candle-light is silvery on her chill bright screen.
Her little silk fan is for fireflies. . . .
She lies watching her staircase cold in the moon,
And two stars parted by the River of Heaven.

(96)

PARTING

I

She is slim and supple and not yet fourteen,
The young spring-tip of a cardamon-spray.
On the Yang-chou Road for three miles in the breeze
Every pearl-screen is open. But there's no one like her.

II

How can a deep love seem deep love,
How can it smile, at a farewell feast?
Even the candle, feeling our sadness,
Weeps, as we do, all night long.

THE GARDEN OF THE GOLDEN VALLEY

Stories of passion make sweet dust,
Calm water, grasses unconcerned.
At sunset, when birds cry in the wind,
Petals are falling like a girl's robe long ago.

(97)

A NIGHT AT A TAVERN

Solitary at the tavern,
I am shut in with loneliness and grief.
Under the cold lamp, I brood on the past;
I am kept awake by a lost wildgoose.
. . . Roused at dawn from a misty dream,
I read, a year late, news from home —
And I remember the moon like smoke on the river
And a fisher-boat moored there, under my door.

(98)

Tu Shên-yen

言審杜

ON A WALK IN THE EARLY SPRING
HARMONIZING A POEM BY MY FRIEND LU
STATIONED AT CH'ANG-CHOU

Only to wanderers can come
Ever new the shock of beauty,
Of white cloud and red cloud dawning from the sea,
Of spring in the wild-plum and river-willow. . . .
I watch a yellow oriole dart in the warm air,
And a green water-plant reflected by the sun.
Suddenly an old song fills
My heart with home, my eyes with tears.

(99, 9)

Wang Ch'ang-ling
齡昌王

AT HIBISCUS INN
PARTING WITH HSIN CHIEN

With this cold night-rain hiding the river, you have come into Wu.
In the level dawn, all alone, you will be starting for the mountains
 of Ch'u.
Answer, if they ask of me at Lo-yang:
"One-hearted as ice in a crystal vase."

IN HER QUIET WINDOW

Too young to have learned what sorrow means,
Attired for spring, she climbs to her high chamber. . . .
The new green of the street-willows is wounding her
 heart —
Just for a title she sent him to war.

A SONG OF THE SPRING PALACE

Last night, while a gust blew peach-petals open
And the moon shone high on the Palace Beyond Time,
The Emperor gave P'ing-yang, for her dancing,
Brocades against the cold spring-wind.

(93)

A SIGH IN THE COURT OF PERPETUAL FAITH
(*Written to Music*)

She brings a broom at dawn to the Golden Palace doorway
And dusts the hall from end to end with her round fan,
And, for all her jade-whiteness, she envies a crow
Whose cold wings are kindled in the Court of the Bright Sun.

(100)

OVER THE BORDER
(*Written to Music*)

The moon goes back to the time of Ch'in, the wall to the time
    of Han,
And the road our troops are travelling goes back three hundred
    miles. . . .
Oh, for the Winged General at the Dragon City —
That never a Tartar horseman might cross the Yin Mountains!

(59)

WITH MY BROTHER AT THE SOUTH STUDY
Thinking in the Moonlight of Vice-Prefect Ts'uêi in Shan-yin

Lying on a high seat in the south study,
We have lifted the curtain — and we see the rising moon
Brighten with pure light the water and the grove
And flow like a wave on our window and our door.
It will move through the cycle, full moon and then crescent again,
Calmly, beyond our wisdom, altering new to old.
. . . Our chosen one, our friend, is now by a limpid river —
Singing, perhaps, a plaintive eastern song.
He is far, far away from us, three hundred miles away.
And yet a breath of orchids comes along the wind.

(101)

AT A BORDER-FORTRESS
(*Written to Music*)

Cicadas complain of thin mulberry-trees
In the Eighth-month chill at the frontier pass.
Through the gate and back again, all along the road,
There is nothing anywhere but yellow reeds and grasses
And the bones of soldiers from Yu and from Ping
Who have buried their lives in the dusty sand.
. . . Let never a cavalier stir you to envy
With boasts of his horse and his horsemanship.

UNDER A BORDER-FORTRESS
(*Written to Music*)

Drink, my horse, while we cross the autumn water!—
The stream is cold and the wind like a sword,
As we watch against the sunset on the sandy plain,
Far, far away, shadowy Ling-t'ao.
Old battles, waged by those long walls,
Once were proud on all men's tongues.
But antiquity now is a yellow dust,
Confusing in the grasses its ruins and white bones.

Wang Chien
建 王

A BRIDE

On the third day, taking my place to cook,
Washing my hands to make the bridal soup,
I decide that not my mother-in-law
But my husband's young sister shall have the first taste.

Wang Chih-huan
汪之王

AT HERON LODGE

Mountains cover the white sun,
And oceans drain the golden river;
But you widen your view three hundred miles
By going up one flight of stairs.

BEYOND THE BORDER
A SONG OF LIANG-CHOU

Where a yellow river climbs to the white clouds,
Near the one city-wall among ten-thousand-foot mountains,
A Tartar under the willows is lamenting on his flute
That spring never blows to him through the Jade Pass.

(102)

Wang Han

翰 王

A SONG OF LIANG-CHOU

They sing, they drain their cups of jade,
They strum on horseback their guitars.
. . . Why laugh when they fall asleep drunk on the sand? —
How many soldiers ever come home?

Wang Po

勃 王

FAREWELL TO VICE-PREFECT TU
SETTING OUT FOR HIS OFFICIAL POST IN SHU

By this wall that surrounds the three Ch'in districts,
Through a mist that makes five rivers one,
We bid each other a sad farewell,
We two officials going opposite ways. . . .
And yet, while China holds our friendship,
And heaven remains our neighbourhood,
Why should you linger at the fork of the road,
Wiping your eyes like a heart-broken child?

Wang Wan

A MOORING UNDER NORTH FORT HILL

Under blue mountains we wound our way,
My boat and I, along green water;
Until the banks at low tide widened,
With no wind stirring my lone sail.
. . . Night now yields to a sea of sun,
And the old year melts in freshets.
At last I can send my messengers —
Wildgeese, homing to Lo-yang.

Wang Wêi

維 王

DEER-PARK HERMITAGE

There seems to be no one on the empty mountain . . .
And yet I think I hear a voice,
Where sunlight, entering a grove,
Shines back to me from the green moss.

(103)

IN A RETREAT AMONG BAMBOOS

Leaning alone in the close bamboos,
I am playing my lute and humming a song
Too softly for anyone to hear —
Except my comrade, the bright moon.

A PARTING

Friend, I have watched you down the mountain
Till now in the dark I close my thatch door. . . .
Grasses return again green in the spring,
But O my Prince of Friends, do you?

(68)

ONE-HEARTED

When those red berries come in springtime,
Flushing on your southland branches,
Take home an armful, for my sake,
As a symbol of our love.

LINES

You who have come from my old country,
Tell me what has happened there! —
Was the plum, when you passed my silken window,
Opening its first cold blossom?

ON THE MOUNTAIN HOLIDAY
THINKING OF MY BROTHERS IN SHAN-TUNG

All alone in a foreign land,
I am twice as homesick on this day
When brothers carry dogwood up the mountain,
Each of them a branch — and my branch missing.

(64)

A SONG AT WÊI-CH'ÊNG
(*Written to Music*)

A morning-rain has settled the dust in Wêi-ch'êng;
Willows are green again in the tavern dooryard. . . .
Wait till we empty one more cup —
West of Yang Gate there'll be no old friends.

(104)

A SONG OF AN AUTUMN NIGHT
(*Written to Music*)

Under the crescent moon a light autumn dew
Has chilled the robe she will not change —
And she touches a silver lute all night,
Afraid to go back to her empty room.

A MESSAGE FROM MY LODGE AT
WANG-CH'ÜAN
To P'AI TI

The mountains are cold and blue now
And the autumn waters have run all day.
By my thatch door, leaning on my staff,
I listen to cicadas in the evening wind.

Sunset lingers at the ferry,
Supper-smoke floats up from the houses.
. . . Oh, when shall I pledge the great Hermit again
And sing a wild poem at Five Willows?

(34, 2a)

AN AUTUMN EVENING IN THE MOUNTAINS

After rain the empty mountain
Stands autumnal in the evening,
Moonlight in its groves of pine,
Stones of crystal in its brooks.
Bamboos whisper of washer-girls bound home,
Lotus-leaves yield before a fisher-boat —
And what does it matter that springtime has gone,
While you are here, O Prince of Friends?

(68)

BOUND HOME TO MOUNT SUNG

The limpid river, past its bushes
Running slowly as my chariot,
Becomes a fellow voyager
Returning home with the evening birds.
A ruined city-wall overtops an old ferry,

Autumn sunset floods the peaks.
. . . Far away, beside Mount Sung,
I shall close my door and be at peace.

(14)

MOUNT CHUNG-NAN

Its massive height near the City of Heaven
Joins a thousand mountains to the corner of the sea.
Clouds, when I look back, close behind me,
Mists, when I enter them, are gone.
A central peak divides the wilds
And weather into many valleys.
. . . Needing a place to spend the night,
I call to a wood-cutter over the river.

(32)

ANSWERING VICE-PREFECT CHANG

As the years go by, give me but peace,
Freedom from ten thousand matters.
I ask myself and always answer:
What can be better than coming home?
A wind from the pine-trees blows my sash,
And my lute is bright with the mountain moon.
You ask me about good and evil fortune? . . .
Hark, on the lake there's a fisherman singing!

TOWARD THE TEMPLE OF HEAPED FRAGRANCE

Not knowing the way to the Temple of Heaped Fragrance,
Under miles of mountain-cloud I have wandered
Through ancient woods without a human track;
But now on the height I hear a bell.
A rillet sings over winding rocks,
The sun is tempered by green pines. . . .
And at twilight, close to an emptying pool,
Thought can conquer the Passion-Dragon.

A MESSAGE TO COMMISSIONER LI
AT TSŬ-CHOU

From ten thousand valleys the trees touch heaven;
On a thousand peaks cuckoos are calling;
And, after a night of mountain rain,
From each summit come hundreds of silken cascades.
. . . If girls are asked in tribute the fibre they weave,
Or farmers quarrel over taro fields,
Preside as wisely as Wên-wêng did. . . .
Is fame to be only for the ancients?

(105)

A VIEW OF THE HAN RIVER

With its three southern branches reaching the Ch'u border,
And its nine streams touching the gateway of Ching,
This river runs beyond heaven and earth,
Where the colour of mountains both is and is not.
The dwellings of men seem floating along
On ripples of the distant sky —
These beautiful days here in Hsiang-yang
Make drunken my old mountain heart!

MY RETREAT AT MOUNT CHUNG-NAN

My heart in middle age found the Way,
And I came to dwell at the foot of this mountain.
When the spirit moves, I wander alone
Amid beauty that is all for me. . . .
I will walk till the water checks my path,
Then sit and watch the rising clouds —
And some day meet an old wood-cutter
And talk and laugh and never return.

(32, 75)

AN EARLY AUDIENCE AT THE PALACE OF LIGHT

HARMONIZING SECRETARY CHIA CHIH'S POEM

The red-capped Cock-Man has just announced morning;
The Keeper of the Robes brings Jade-Cloud Furs;
Heaven's nine doors reveal the palace and its courtyards;
And the coats of many countries bow to the Pearl Crown.
Sunshine has entered the giants' carven palms;
Incense wreathes the Dragon Robe:
The audience adjourns — and the five-coloured edict
Sets girdle-beads clinking toward the Lake of the Phœnix.

(9, 9a, 106)

LOOKING DOWN IN A SPRING-RAIN ON THE COURSE FROM FAIRY-MOUNTAIN PALACE TO THE PAVILION OF INCREASE

HARMONIZING THE EMPEROR'S POEM

Round a turn of the Ch'in Fortress winds the Wêi River,
And Yellow Mountain foot-hills enclose the Court of China;
Past the South Gate willows comes the Car of Many Bells
On the upper Palace-Garden Road — a solid length of blossom;
A Forbidden City roof holds two phœnixes in cloud;

The foliage of spring shelters multitudes from rain;
And now, when the heavens are propitious for action,
Here is our Emperor ready — no wasteful wanderer.

(4ª, 9)

IN MY LODGE AT WANG-CH'ÜAN
AFTER A LONG RAIN

The woods have stored the rain, and slow comes the smoke
As rice is cooked on faggots and carried to the fields;
Over the quiet marsh-land flies a white egret,
And mango-birds are singing in the full summer trees. . . .
I have learned to watch in peace the mountain morning-glories,
To eat split dewy sunflower-seeds under a bough of pine,
To yield the post of honour to any boor at all . . .
Why should I frighten sea-gulls, even with a thought?

(107)

HARMONIZING A POEM BY
PALACE-ATTENDANT KUO

High beyond the thick wall a tower shines with sunset
Where peach and plum are blooming and the willow-cotton flies.
You have heard in your office the court-bell of twilight;
Birds find perches, officials head for home.

Your morning-jade will tinkle as you thread the golden palace;
You will bring the word of Heaven from the closing gates at night.
And I should serve there with you; but being full of years,
I have taken off official robes and am resting from my troubles.

(9)

AT PARTING

I dismount from my horse and I offer you wine,
And I ask you where you are going and why.
And you answer: " I am discontent
And would rest at the foot of the southern mountain.
So give me leave and ask me no questions.
White clouds pass there without end."

TO CHI-WU CH'IEN BOUND HOME
AFTER FAILING IN AN EXAMINATION

In a happy reign there should be no hermits;
The wise and able should consult together. . . .
So you, a man of the eastern mountains,
Gave up your life of picking herbs
And came all the way to the Gate of Gold —
But you found your devotion unavailing.
. . . To spend the Day of No Fire on one of the southern rivers,
You have mended your spring clothes here in these northern cities.

I pour you the farewell wine as you set out from the capital —
Soon I shall be left behind here by my bosom-friend.
In your sail-boat of sweet cinnamon-wood
You will float again toward your own thatch door,
Led along by distant trees
To a sunset shining on a far-away town.
. . . What though your purpose happened to fail,
Doubt not that some of us can hear high music.

(1, 54)

A GREEN STREAM

I have sailed the River of Yellow Flowers,
Borne by the channel of a green stream,
Rounding ten thousand turns through the mountains
On a journey of less than thirty miles. . . .
Rapids hum over heaped rocks;
But where light grows dim in the thick pines,
The surface of an inlet sways with nut-horns
And weeds are lush along the banks.
. . . Down in my heart I have always been as pure
As this limpid water is. . . .
Oh, to remain on a broad flat rock
And to cast a fishing-line forever!

A FARM-HOUSE ON THE WÊI RIVER

In the slant of the sun on the country-side,
Cattle and sheep trail home along the lane;
And a rugged old man in a thatch door
Leans on a staff and thinks of his son, the herd-boy.
There are whirring pheasants, full wheat-ears,
Silk-worms asleep, pared mulberry-leaves.
And the farmers, returning with hoes on their shoulders,
Hail one another familiarly.
. . . No wonder I long for the simple life
And am sighing the old song, *Oh, to go Back Again!*

(108)

THE BEAUTIFUL HSI SHIH

Since beauty is honoured all over the Empire,
How could Hsi Shih remain humbly at home? —
Washing clothes at dawn by a southern lake —
And that evening a great lady in a palace of the north:
Lowly one day, no different from the others,
The next day exalted, everyone praising her.
No more would her own hands powder her face
Or arrange on her shoulders a silken robe.
And the more the King loved her, the lovelier she looked,
Blinding him away from wisdom.

... Girls who had once washed silk beside her
Were kept at a distance from her chariot.
And none of the girls in her neighbours' houses
By pursing their brows could copy her beauty.

(109)

A SONG OF A GIRL FROM LO-YANG
(*Written to Music*)

There's a girl from Lo-yang in the door across the street,
She looks fifteen, she may be a little older.
... While her master rides his rapid horse with jade bit and
bridle,
Her handmaid brings her cod-fish in a golden plate.
On her painted pavilions, facing red towers,
Cornices are pink and green with peach-bloom and with willow.
Canopies of silk awn her seven-scented chair,
And rare fans shade her, home to her nine-flowered curtains.
Her lord, with rank and wealth and in the bud of life,
Exceeds in munificence the richest men of old.
He favours this girl of lowly birth, he has her taught to dance;
And he gives away his coral-trees to almost anyone.
The wind of dawn just stirs when his nine soft lights go out,
Those nine soft lights like petals in a flying chain of flowers.
Between dances she has barely time for singing over the songs;
No sooner is she dressed again than incense burns before her.
Those she knows in town are only the rich and the lavish,

And day and night she is visiting the hosts of the gayest mansions.
. . . Who notices the girl from Yüeh with a face of white jade,
Humble, poor, alone, by the river, washing silk?

(110)

A SONG OF AN OLD GENERAL
(*Written to Music*)

When he was a youth of fifteen or twenty,
He chased a wild horse, he caught him and rode him,
He shot the white-browed mountain tiger,
He defied the yellow-bristled Horseman of Yieh.
Fighting single-handed for a thousand miles,
With his naked dagger he could hold a multitude.
. . . Granted that the troops of China were as swift as heaven's
    thunder
And that Tartar soldiers perished in pitfalls fanged with iron,
General Wêi Ch'ing's victory was only a thing of chance.
And General Li Kuang's thwarted effort was his fate, not his fault.
Since this man's retirement he is looking old and worn:
Experience of the world has hastened his white hairs.
Though once his quick dart never missed the right eye of a bird,
Now knotted veins and tendons make his left arm like an osier.
He is sometimes at the road-side selling melons from his garden,
He is sometimes planting willows round his hermitage.
His lonely lane is shut away by a dense grove,
His vacant window looks upon the far cold mountains. . . .
But, if he prayed, the waters would come gushing for his men

And never would he wanton his cause away with wine.

. . . War-clouds are spreading, under the Ho-lan Range;

Back and forth, day and night, go feathered messages;

In the three River Provinces, the governors call young men —

And five imperial edicts have summoned the old general.

So he dusts his iron coat and shines it like snow —

Waves his dagger from its jade hilt in a dance of starry steel.

He is ready with his strong northern bow to smite the Tartar chieftain —

That never a foreign war-dress may affront the Emperor.

. . . There once was an aged Prefect, forgotten and far away,

Who still could manage triumph with a single stroke.

(III)

A SONG OF PEACH-BLOSSOM RIVER

(*Written to Music*)

A fisherman is drifting, enjoying the spring mountains,

And the peach-trees on both banks lead him to an ancient source.

Watching the fresh-coloured trees, he never thinks of distance

Till he comes to the end of the blue stream and suddenly — strange men!

It's a cave — with a mouth so narrow that he has to crawl through;

But then it opens wide again on a broad and level path —

And far beyond he faces clouds crowning a reach of trees,

And thousands of houses shadowed round with flowers and bamboos. . . .

Woodsmen tell him their names in the ancient speech of Han;

And clothes of the Ch'in Dynasty are worn by all these people
Living on the uplands, above the Wu-ling River,
On farms and in gardens that are like a world apart,
Their dwellings at peace under pines in the clear moon,
Until sunrise fills the low sky with crowing and barking.
. . . At news of a stranger the people all assemble,
And each of them invites him home and asks him where he was
    born.
Alleys and paths are cleared for him of petals in the morning,
And fishermen and farmers bring him their loads at dusk. . . .
They had left the world long ago, they had come here seeking
    refuge;
They have lived like angels ever since, blessedly far away,
No one in the cave knowing anything outside,
Outsiders viewing only empty mountains and thick clouds.
. . . The fisherman, unaware of his great good fortune,
Begins to think of country, of home, of worldly ties,
Finds his way out of the cave again, past mountains and past
    rivers,
Intending some time to return, when he has told his kin.
He studies every step he takes, fixes it well in mind,
And forgets that cliffs and peaks may vary their appearance.
. . . It is certain that to enter through the deepness of the
    mountain,
A green river leads you, into a misty wood.
But now, with spring-floods everywhere and floating peach-
    petals —
Which is the way to go, to find that hidden source?
(2)

Wêi Chuang

莊 韋

A NAN-KING LANDSCAPE

Though a shower bends the river-grass, a bird is singing,
While ghosts of the Six Dynasties pass like a dream
Around the Forbidden City, under weeping willows
Which loom still for three miles along the misty moat.

(112)

A NIGHT THOUGHT ON TERRACE TOWER

Far through the night a harp is sighing
With a sadness of wind and rain in the strings. . . .
There's a solitary lantern, a bugle-call —
And beyond Terrace Tower down goes the moon.
. . . Fragrant grasses have changed and faded
While still I have been hoping that my old friend would come. . . .
There are no more messengers I can send him,
Now that the wildgeese have turned south.

(39a)

Wêi Ying-wu

物應韋

AN AUTUMN NIGHT MESSAGE
To Ch'iu

As I walk in the cool of the autumn night,
Thinking of you, singing my poem,
I hear a mountain pine-cone fall. . . .
You also seem to be awake.

AT CH'U-CHOU ON THE WESTERN STREAM

Where tender grasses rim the stream
And deep boughs trill with mango-birds,
On the spring flood of last night's rain
The ferry-boat moves as though someone were poling.

(113)

A GREETING ON THE HUAI RIVER
TO MY OLD FRIENDS FROM LIANG-CH'ÜAN

We used to be companions on the Kiang and the Han,
And as often as we met, we were likely to be tipsy.
Since we left one another, floating apart like clouds,
Ten years have run like water — till at last we join again.
And we talk again and laugh again just as in earlier days,
Except that the hair on our heads is tinged now with grey. . . .
Why not come along, then, all of us together,
And face the autumn mountains and sail along the Huai?

A FAREWELL IN THE EVENING RAIN
To Li Ts'ao

Is it raining on the river all the way to Ch'u? —
The evening bell comes to us from Nan-king.
Your wet sail drags and is loath to be going
And shadowy birds are flying slow.
We cannot see the deep ocean-gate —
Only the boughs at Pu-kou, newly dripping.
Likewise, because of our great love,
There are threads of water on our faces.

TO MY FRIENDS LI TAN AND YÜAN HSI

We met last among flowers, among flowers we parted,
And here, a year later, there are flowers again;
But, with ways of the world too strange to foretell,
Spring only brings me grief and fatigue.
I am sick, and I think of my home in the country —
Ashamed to take pay while so many are idle.
. . . In my western tower, because of your promise,
I have watched the full moons come and go.

ENTERTAINING LITERARY MEN
IN MY OFFICIAL RESIDENCE
ON A RAINY DAY

Outside are insignia, shown in state;
But here are sweet incense-clouds, quietly ours.
Wind and rain, coming in from sea,
Have cooled this pavilion above the lake
And driven the feverish heat away
From where my eminent guests are gathered.
. . . Ashamed though I am of my high position
While people lead unhappy lives,
Let us reasonably banish care
And just be friends, enjoying nature.
Though we have to go without fish and meat,
There are fruits and vegetables aplenty.

. . . We bow, we take our cups of wine,
We give our attention to beautiful poems.
When the mind is exalted, the body is lightened
And feels as if it could float in the wind.
. . . Su-chou is famed as a centre of letters;
And all you writers, coming here,
Prove that the name of a great land
Is made by better things than wealth.

SETTING SAIL ON THE YANG-TSZE
To Secretary Yüan

Wistful, away from my friends and kin,
Through mist and fog I float and float
With the sail that bears me toward Lo-yang.
In Yang-chou trees linger bell-notes of evening,
Marking the day and the place of our parting. . . .
When shall we meet again and where?
. . . Destiny is a boat on the waves,
Borne to and fro, beyond our will.

A POEM TO A TAOIST HERMIT
ON CH'ÜAN-CHIAO MOUNTAIN

My office has grown cold today;
And I suddenly think of my mountain friend
Gathering firewood down in the valley

Or boiling white stones for potatoes in his hut . . .
I wish I might take him a cup of wine
To cheer him through the evening storm;
But in fallen leaves that have heaped the bare slopes,
How should I ever find his footprints!

(62a)

ON MEETING MY FRIEND FÊNG CHU
IN THE CAPITAL

Out of the east you visit me,
With the rain of Pa-ling still on your clothes,
I ask you what you have come here for;
You say: "To buy an ax for cutting wood in the mountains."
. . . Hidden deep in a haze of blossom,
Swallow fledglings chirp at ease
As they did when we parted, a year ago. . . .
How grey our temples have grown since then!

MOORING AT TWILIGHT IN YÜ-YI DISTRICT

Furling my sail near the town of Huai,
I find for harbour a little cove
Where a sudden breeze whips up the waves.
. . . The sun is growing dim now and sinks in the dusk.

People are coming home. The bright mountain-peak darkens.
Wildgeese fly down to an island of white weeds.
. . . At midnight I think of a northern city-gate,
And I hear a bell tolling between me and sleep.

EAST OF THE TOWN

From office confinement all year long,
I have come out of town to be free this morning
Where willows harmonize the wind
And green hills lighten the cares of the world.
I lean by a tree and rest myself
Or wander up and down a stream.
. . . Mists have wet the fragrant meadows;
A spring dove calls from some hidden place.
. . . With quiet surroundings, the mind is at peace,
But beset with affairs, it grows restless again . . .
Here I shall finally build me a cabin,
As T'ao Ch'ien built one long ago.

(2a)

TO MY DAUGHTER
ON HER MARRIAGE INTO THE YANG FAMILY

My heart has been heavy all day long
Because you have so far to go.
The marriage of a girl, away from her parents,

Is the launching of a little boat on a great river.
. . . You were very young when your mother died,
Which made me the more tender of you.
Your elder sister has looked out for you,
And now you are both crying and cannot part.
This makes my grief the harder to bear;
Yet it is right that you should go.
. . . Having had from childhood no mother to guide you,
How will you honour your mother-in-law?
It's an excellent family; they will be kind to you,
They will forgive you your mistakes —
Although ours has been so pure and poor
That you can take them no great dowry.
Be gentle and respectful, as a woman should be,
Careful of word and look, observant of good example.
. . . After this morning we separate,
There's no knowing for how long . . .
I always try to hide my feelings —
They are suddenly too much for me,
When I turn and see my younger daughter
With the tears running down her cheek.

Wên T'ing-yun
筠庭溫

SHE SIGHS ON HER JADE LUTE

A cool-matted silvery bed; but no dreams. . . .
An evening sky as green as water, shadowed with tender clouds;
But far off over the southern rivers the calling of a wildgoose,
And here a twelve-story building, lonely under the moon.

TO A FRIEND BOUND EAST

The old fort brims with yellow leaves. . . .
You insist upon forsaking this place where you have lived.
A high wind blows at Han-yang Ferry
And sunrise lights the summit of Ying-mên . . .
Who will be left for me along the upper Yang-tsze
After your solitary skiff has entered the end of the sky?
I ask you over and over when we shall meet again,
While we soften with winecups this ache of farewell.

NEAR THE LI-CHOU FERRY

The sun has set in the water's clear void,
And little blue islands are one with the sky.
On the bank a horse neighs. A boat goes by.
People gather at a willow-clump and wait for the ferry.
Down by the sand-bushes sea-gulls are circling,
Over the wide river-lands flies an egret.
. . . Can you guess why I sail, like an ancient wise lover,
Through the misty Five Lakes, forgetting words?

(109)

THE TEMPLE OF SU WU

Though our envoy, Su Wu, is gone, body and soul,
This temple survives, these trees endure . . .
Wildgeese through the clouds are still calling to the moon there
And hill-sheep unshepherded graze along the border.
. . . Returning, he found his country changed
Since with youthful cap and sword he had left it.
His bitter adventures had won him no title . . .
Autumn-waves endlessly sob in the river.

(114)

Yüan Chên

稹 元

THE SUMMER PALACE

In the faded old imperial palace,
Peonies are red, but no one comes to see them. . . .
The ladies-in-waiting have grown white-haired
Debating the pomps of Emperor Hsüan-tsung.

(4d)

AN ELEGY

I

O youngest, best-loved daughter of Hsieh,
Who unluckily married this penniless scholar,
You patched my clothes from your own wicker basket,
And I coaxed off your hairpins of gold, to buy wine with;
For dinner we had to pick wild herbs —
And to use dry locust-leaves for our kindling.
. . . Today they are paying me a hundred thousand —
And all that I can bring to you is a temple sacrifice.

II

We joked, long ago, about one of us dying,
But suddenly, before my eyes, you are gone.
Almost all your clothes have been given away;
Your needlework is sealed, I dare not look at it. . . .
I continue your bounty to our men and our maids —
Sometimes, in a dream, I bring you gifts.
. . . This is a sorrow that all mankind must know —
But not as those know it who have been poor together.

III

I sit here alone, mourning for us both.
How many years do I lack now of my threescore and ten?
There have been better men than I to whom heaven denied a son,
There was a poet better than I whose dead wife could not hear
    him.
What have I to hope for in the darkness of our tomb?
You and I had little faith in a meeting after death —
Yet my open eyes can see all night
That lifelong trouble of your brow.

(115)

Yüan Chieh

結 元

TO THE TAX-COLLECTORS
AFTER THE BANDITS' RETREAT

(In the year Kuêi-mao the bandits from Hsi-yüan entered Tao-chou, set fire, raided, killed, and looted. The whole district was almost ruined. The next year the bandits came again and, attacking the neighbouring prefecture, Yüng, passed this one by. It was not because we were strong enough to defend ourselves, but, probably, because they pitied us. And how now can these commissioners bear to impose extra taxes? I have written this poem for the collectors' information.)

I still remember those days of peace —
Twenty years among mountains and forests,
The pure stream running past my yard,
The caves and valleys at my door.
Taxes were light and regular then,
And I could sleep soundly and late in the morning —
Till suddenly came a sorry change.
. . . For years now I have been serving in the army.
When I began here as an official,
The mountain bandits were rising again;
But the town was so small it was spared by the thieves,
And the people so poor and so pitiable

That all the other districts were looted
And this one this time let alone.
. . . Do you imperial commissioners
Mean to be less kind than bandits?
The people you force to pay the poll
Are like creatures frying over a fire.
And how can you sacrifice human lives,
Just to be known as able collectors? —
. . . Oh, let me fling down my official seal,
Let me be a lone fisherman in a small boat
And support my family on fish and wheat
And content my old age with rivers and lakes!

A DRINKING SONG AT STONE-FISH LAKE

(I have used grain from the public fields, for distilling wine. After my office hours I have the wine loaded on a boat and then I seat my friends on the bank of the lake. The little wine-boats come to each of us and supply us with wine. We seem to be drinking on Pa Islet in Lake Tung-t'ing. And I write this poem.)

Stone-Fish Lake is like Lake Tung-t'ing —
When the top of Chün is green and the summer tide is rising.
. . . With the mountain for a table, and the lake a fount of wine,
The tipplers all are settled along the sandy shore.
Though a stiff wind for days has roughened the water,
Wine-boats constantly arrive. . . .
I have a long-necked gourd and, happy on Pa Island,
I am pouring a drink in every direction, doing away with care.

Appendices

HISTORICAL CHRONOLOGY

I

The Five Ti Periods, 2953–2206
The Hsia Dynasty, 2205–1766
The Shang Dynasty, 1765–1122
The Chou Dynasty, 1121–256
The Ch'in Dynasty, 255–207
The Han Dynasty, 206–219
The Three Kingdoms Period, 220–264
The Chin Dynasty, 265–419
The Southern and Northern Dynasties, 420–588
The Suêi Dynasty, 589–617
The T'ang Dynasty, 618–906
The Five Dynasties, 907–959
The Sung Dynasty, 960–1279
The Liao and Chin Tartar Dynasties, 916–1234
The Yuan or Mongol Dynasty, 1280–1367
The Ming Dynasty, 1368–1643
The Ch'ing or Manchu Dynasty, 1644–1911

II

THE T'ANG DYNASTY

1. Emperor Kao-tsu, Wu-tê Period, 618–626
2. Emperor T'ai-tsung, Chêng-kuan Period, 627–649

3. Emperor Kao-tsung, Yung-huêi Period, 650–655
    Hsien-ch'ing Period, 656–660
    Lung-so Period, 661–663
    Lin-tê Period, 664–665
    Ch'ien-fêng Period, 666–667
    Tsung-chang Period, 668–669
    Hsien-hêng Period, 670–673
    Shang-yuan Period, 674–675
    Yi-fêng Period, 676–678
    T'iao-lu Period, 679
    Yung-lung Period, 680
    K'ai-yao Period, 681
    Yung-shun Period, 682
    Hung-tao Period, 683
4. Emperor Chung-tsung, Ssŭ-shêng Period, 684
5. Emperor Juêi-tsung, Ch'uêi-kung Period, 685–688
6. The Woman Emperor Wu-chao, T'ien-shou Period, 690–691
    Ju-yi Period, 692
    Ch'ang-shou Period, 693
    Yen-tsai Period, 694
    T'ien-ts'e-wan-suêi Period, 695
    Wan-suêi-t'ung-t'ien Period, 696
    Shên-kung Period, 697
    Shêng-li Period, 698–699
    Chiu-shih Period, 700
    Ch'ang-an Period, 701–704
7. Emperor Chung-tsung restored, Shên-lung Period, 705–706
    Chin-lung Period, 707–709

8. Emperor Juêi-tsung, Ching-yun Period, 710–711
      Hsien-t'ien Period, 712

9. Emperor Hsüan-tsung, K'ai-yuan Period, 713–741
      T'ien-pao Period, 742–755

10. Emperor Su-tsung, Chih Tê Period, 756–757
      Ch'ien-yuan Period, 758–759
      Shang-yuan Period, 760–761
      Pao-yin Period, 762

11. Emperor Tai-tsung, Kuang-tê Period, 763–764
      Yung-t'ai Period, 765
      Ta-li Period, 766–779

12. Emperor Tê-tsung, Chien-chung Period, 780–783
      Hsing-yuan Period, 784
      Cheng-yuan Period, 785–804

13. Emperor Shun-tsung, Yung-cheng Period, 805

14. Emperor Hsien-tsung, Yuan-ho Period, 806–820

15. Emperor Mu-tsung, Ch'ang-ch'ing Period, 821–824

16. Emperor Ching-tsung, Pao-li Period, 825–826

17. Emperor Wên-tsung, T'ai-ho Period, 827–835
      K'ai-ch'eng Period, 836–840

18. Emperor Wu-tsung, Huêi-ch'ang Period, 841–846

19. Emperor Hsüan-tsung, Ta-chung Period, 847–859

20. Emperor Yi-tsung, Hsien-tung Period, 860–873

21. Emperor Hsi-tsung, Ch'ien-fu Period, 874–879
      Kuang-ming Period, 880
      Chung-ho Period, 881–884
      Kuang-ch'i Period, 885–887
      Wên Tê Period, 888

22. Emperor Chao-tsung, Lung-chi Period, 889
       Ta-shun Period, 890–891
       Ch'ing-fu Period, 892–893
       Ch'ien-ning Period, 894–897
       Kuang-hua Period, 898–900
       T'ien-fu Period, 901–903
       T'ien-yu Period, 904–906

CHRONOLOGY OF THE POETS

Names		*Dates*
Anonymous	無名氏	
Chang Chi (1)	張 繼	Graduated [1] between 742 and 755, lived to 780
Chang Chi (2)	張 籍	Graduated 799
Chang Ch'iao	張 喬	Graduated about 870
Ch'ang Chien	常 建	Graduated 727
Chang Chiu-ling	張 九 齡	673–740
Chang Hsü	張 旭	Early 8th century
Chang Hu	張 祜	9th century
Chang Pi	張 泌	10th century
Ch'ên T'ao	陳 陶	824–882
Ch'ên Tzŭ-ang	陳 子 昂	656–698
Chêng T'ien	鄭 畋	656–698
Chia Tao	賈 島	788–843
Ch'ien Ch'i	錢 起	Graduated 751
Chin Ch'ang-hsü	金 昌 緒	10th century
Ch'in T'ao-yü	秦 韜 玉	Graduated 882
Ch'iu Wêi	邱 爲	8th century, died at age 96
Chi-wu Ch'ien	綦 毋 潛	Graduated 726
Chu Ch'ing-yü	朱 慶 餘	Graduated 825

[1] The term "graduated" is used in the sense of receiving an official degree at the government examinations.

Names		Dates
Ch'üan Tê-yü	輿德權	759–818
Han Hung	翃 韓	Graduated 754
Han Wu	偓 韓	Graduated 889, died 905
Han Yü	愈 韓	768–823
Hê Chih-chang	章知賀	659–744
Hsü Hun	渾 許	Graduated 832
Hsüan-tsung, Emperor	宗 玄	685–761, reigned 713–755
Hsüeh Fêng	逢 薛	Graduated about 845
Huang-fu Jan	冉甫皇	714–767
Kao Shih	適 高	Died 765
Ku K'uang	況 顧	Graduated either in 756 or in 757
Li Ch'i	頎 李	Graduated 725
Li P'in	頻 李	Graduated 854
Li Po	白 李	699–762
Li Shang-yin	隱商李	813–858
Li Tuan	端 李	Graduated 770
Li Yi	益 李	Graduated 769, died 827
Liu Chang-ch'ing	卿長劉	Graduated 733
Liu Chung-yung	庸中柳	8th and 9th centuries
Liu Fang-p'ing	平方劉	8th and 9th centuries
Liu Shên-hsü	虛眘劉	Flourished about 742–755
Liu Tsung-yüan	元宗柳	773–819
Liu Yü-hsi	錫禹劉	772–842
Lo Ping-wang	王賓駱	Flourished early 7th century
Ma Tai	戴 馬	Graduated 844

Names		Dates
Mêng Chiao	郊 孟	751–814
Mêng Hao-jan	然浩孟	699–740
One at the Western Front	人鄙西	Unknown
P'ai Ti	迪 裴	9th century
Po Chü-yi	易居白	772–846
Sêng Chiao-jan	然皎僧	Died 785
Shên Ch'uan-ch'i	期佺沈	Graduated about 680, died about 713
Ssǔ-k'ung Shu	曙空司	Flourished 766–779
Sung Chih-wên	問之宋	Died 710
Tai Shu-lun	倫叔戴	732–789
Ts'ên Ts'an	參 岑	Graduated 744
Tsu Yüng	詠 祖	Graduated 724
Ts'uêi Hao	灝 崔	Graduated 723, died 754
Ts'uêi Shu	曙 崔	Graduated in 738
Ts'uêi T'u	塗 崔	Graduated 888
Tu Ch'iu-niang	娘秋杜	Early 9th century
Tu Fu	甫 杜	712–770
Tu Hsün-hê	鶴荀杜	Graduated 891, died about 904
Tu Mu	牧 杜	803–852
Tu Shên-yen	言審杜	Between 7th and 8th centuries
Wang Ch'ang-ling	齡昌王	Graduated 726
Wang Chien	建 王	Graduated 775
Wang Chih-huan	渙之王	8th century

Names			Dates
Wang Han	翰	王	Graduated about 735
Wang Po	勃	王	648–675
Wang Wan	灣	王	Graduated 712
Wang Wêi	維	王	699–759
Wêi Chüang	莊	韋	Graduated 902
Wêi Ying-wu	物應	韋	773–828
Wên T'ing-yün	筠庭	溫	9th century
Yüan Chên	稹	元	799–831
Yüan Chieh	結	元	719–772

TOPOGRAPHY

We have thought it best to substitute now and then in the text of the poems the modern names of places, with an attempt at consistent spelling, for the T'ang names used in the original; sometimes we have indulged in English translations of the names; but this index records the old names, for scholars who may be interested. It also locates in modern geography the towns, lakes, rivers, mountains, and, roughly, the larger regions, for the possible interest of students and travellers. We use, however, the suffix " ou " instead of " ow ": Han-k'ou, Su-chou and Yang-chou, instead of Hankow, Soochow and Yangchow. The T'ang capital, often mentioned in these poems, was Ch'ang-an, now Hsi-an-fu in Shen-si Province. Han was China, and Fan the outside world. The Three Kingdoms (220–264) were Shu, now Sze-chuan Province; Wu, now Kiang-su Province and other provinces in the Yang-tsze valley; and Wêi, now Ho-nan Province and other provinces in the Huang-ho valley.

The T'ang names of regional divisions most important for readers of the poems are, with approximate modern equivalents:

Chin (Shan-si Province)   Wêi (Ho-nan Province)
Ch'in (Shen-si Province)   Wu (Kiang-su Province)
Chu (Hu-nan Province)   Yen (Chih-li Province)
Ping (Shan-si Province)   Yu (Chih-li Province)
Shu (Sze-chuan Province)   Yüeh (Chê-kiang Province).

APPENDICES

General List

Broken Mountain Temple (P'o-shan): in Ch'ang-shu district, Kiang-su Province

Ch'ang-an: the T'ang capital, now Hsi-an-fu, in Shen-si Province

Chang-chou: a district in Fu-kien Province

Ch'ang-chou: a district in Kiang-su Province

Chang-fêng-sha (Wind-swept Sands): in An-huêi Province

Ch'ang-kan: a small town near Nan-king

Chang-sha: the capital of Hu-nan Province

Chao: a district in Chih-li Province

Chêng: a district in Ho-nan Province

Ch'êng-tu (Ching-ch'êng, called the City of Silk): the capital of Sze-chuan Province

Chien-tê: a town and a river in Chê-kiang Province

Chin: Shan-si Province

Ch'in: Shen-si Province

Ching Gate (Ching-mên): at Ching-chou, in Hu-pêi Province

Ch'in-huai River: at Nan-king

Ch'i-yang: in Shen-si Province

Ch'u: Hu-nan Province

Ch'u Mountains: in Hu-nan Province

Ch'u Rivers: the Han and Hsiang Rivers in Hu-pêi and Hu-nan Provinces

Chüan-chiao Mountain: in An-huêi Province

Ch'u-chou: a district in An-huêi Province

Ch'ü-li: in Manchuria

Chung-nan Mountain (Southernmost Mountain): fifteen miles south of Ch'ang-an, one of the Nan-shan Range, in Shen-si Province

Ch'ü-t'ang: the first of the three great gorges on the upper Yang-tsze; also a district in Sze-chuan Province

City of Silk: Chêng-tu, in Sze-chuan Province

Dagger River (Chien-ho): the upper part of the Yang-tsze, in Sin-kiang Province

Dagger-Tower Trail: in Sze-chuan Province

Dragon City (Lung-ch'êng): in Manchuria

Dragon Mound (Lung-tuêi): in Turkestan

Fêng-chi Station: in Sze-chuan Province

Fêng-chou: a district in Kuang-tung Province

Fêng-hsiang: a district in Shen-si Province

Fou-liang: a district in Kiang-si Province

Fu-chou: a district in Shen-si Province

Fu-li: a district in An-huêi Province

Giant's Palm (Hsien-jên-chang): one of the peaks of Great Flower Mountain

Great Flower Mountain (T'ai-hua or Hua-shan): in Shen-si Province

Great White Mountian (T'ai-po): in Sze-chuan Province

Green Clay Mountain (Ch'ing-ni): in Sze-chuan Province

Han: China

Han-k'ou (Hsia-k'ou): in Hu-pêi Province

Han River: joins the Yang-tsze in Hu-pêi Province

Han-yang: in Hu-pêi Province

Heavenly Mother Mountain (T'ien-mu): a peak of the T'ien-t'ai Mountains in Chê-kiang Province

Heavenly Terrace Range (T'ien-t'ai): in Chê-kiang Province

Heaven-Peak Road: on T'ien-shan, in Turkestan

Hêng Mountain: in Hu-nan Province, one of the Five Holy Mountains

Hill of Gold (Chin-shan): between Mongolia and Manchuria

Ho-lan Range: in Kan-su Province, near Turkestan

Hsia-kuêi: a district in Shen-si Province

Hsiang River: in Hu-nan Province

Hsiang-yang: a district in Hu-pêi Province

Hsiao River: in Hu-nan Province

Hsia-yung: a district in Sze-chuan Province

Hsi-yüan: a district in Shen-si Province

Hsüan-chou: a district in An-huêi Province

Hsün-yang River: at Kiu-kiang

Hua-chou: a district in Shen-si Province

Huai: a district in Kiang-su Province

Huai River: a tributary of the Yang-tsze, in Kiang-su Province

Hua-mên tribes: Turkestanese

Hua-yin: the district under T'ai-hua (Great Flower Mountain) and around Hsien-yang, a local T'ang capital, in Shen-si Province

Jade Pass (Yü-mên, Yü-kuan, or Yü-mên-kuan): a gateway or divide between China and Turkestan, now in the western part of Tun-huang district, Kan-su Province

Jo-ya Lake: in Chê-kiang Province

Kiang-ling: a district in Hu-pêi Province

Kiu-kiang (Chiang-chou or Hsün-yang): in Kiang-si Province

Kua-chou: a town in Kiang-su Province, across the Yang-tsze from Chin-kiang

Kuan-nêi: within the Great Wall, in Shen-si Province

Liang-chou: a district in Kan-su Province

Liang-ch'uan: unknown

Liao: near Mukden, Manchuria

Liao-hsi: a border-camp, in Manchuria

Li-chou Ferry: unknown

Liao-yang: a district in Feng-tien Province, Manchuria

Lien-chou: a district in Kuang-tung Province

Li-mien tribes: Manchus

Ling-ch'üng: a district in Sze-chuan Province

Ling-t'ao: a district in Kan-su Province

Ling-t'ao River: between China and Tibet

Ling Valleys: in Shen-si Province

Ling-ying: a district in Ho-nan Province

Liu-chou: in Kuang-si Province

Lo-yang: a district in Ho-nan Province, a principal city of the
T'ang Dynasty, formerly a capital of China

Lo-yu Tombs: in Ch'ang-an (Hsi-an-fu) in Shen-si Province

Lu Dukedom: near T'ai-shan, in Shan-tung Province

Lu-mên: near Hsiang-yang in Hu-pêi Province

Lu Mountain: near Kiu-kiang in Kiang-si Province

Ma-wêi Slope: near Ch'ang-an (Hsi-an-fu) in Shen-si Prov-
ince

Mao-ling: in Hu-nan Province

Maple Bridge (Fêng-ch'iao): in Su-chou, Kiang-su Province

Mêng Valley: in Hu-pêi Province

Mi-lo River: in Hu-nan Province

Mirror Lake (Ching-hu): in Chê-kiang Province

Nan-king (Chin-ling or Chien-yê): in Kiang-su Province

Nan-ling: a district in An-huêi Province

Nine Doubts Mountain (Chiu-ni): in Hu-nan Province

Niu-chu Mountain: on the Yang-tsze not far from An-king, in
An-huêi Province

North Fort Hill (Pêi-ku): in Chin-kiang, Kiang-su Province

O-mêi Mountain: one hundred and seventy miles south-west of
Ch'êng-tu, in Sze-chuan Province

Orchid Mountain (Lan-shan): in Kan-su Province

Pa: a district in Sze-chuan Province

Pa-ling: a district in Shen-si Province

Pa Island: in Hu-nan Province

Parrot Island (Ying-wu-chou): near Han-kou, Hu-pêi Prov-
ince

Pa-shang: near Ch'ang-an (Hsi-an-fu), Shen-si Province

P'en-p'u: in Kiu-kiang, Kiang-si Province

Persia: Chiu-tzŭ

Ping: Shan-si Province

Po-têng Road: in Manchuria

Po-ti (the City of the White God): in Sze-chuan Province

Pu-kou: in Kiang-su Province

Red Phœnix City: Ch'ang-an

Running Horse River (Tsou-ma-ch'uan): in Manchuria

Sand Mouth (Sha-k'ou): in Turkestan

San-yuan (Yün-yang): a district in Shen-si Province

Shan-yin: a district in Chê-kiang Province

Shin-fêng: a place in Ch'ang-kan; also a district in Kiang-su
Province

Shou-hsiang: a border-city near Mount Hui-lo in Manchuria

Shu: Sze-chuan Province

Siberia: Lo-so

Stone-Fish Lake (Shih-yŭ-hu): in An-huêi Province

Su-chou (Ku-su): in Kiang-su Province

Sung Mountain: near Lo-yang, in Ho-nan Province, one of the Five Holy Mountains

T'ai-shan: the Holy Mountain, in Shan-tung Province

Tao-chou: a district in Hu-nan Province

Ta-yü Mountain: between Kiang-si and Kuang-tung Provinces

Terrace Tower: a part of the Nan-king city-wall

Tibet: Yüeh-chih

Ting-chou: a district in Fu-kien Province

Town of the Horse (Ma-yi): in Turkestan

Tripod Fall (Hsiang-lu): one of the peaks of Lu Mountain, in Kiang-si Province

Tsou Realm: near T'ai-shan, in Shan-tung Province

Tsŭ-chou: in Sze-chuan Province

T'ung Gate (T'ung-kuan): a gate or pass by the T'ung River, in Shen-si Province

T'ung-lu River: in An-huêi Province

Tung-t'ing Lake: between Hu-nan and Hu-pêi Provinces

Turkestan (T'u-chüeh): Sin-kiang Province

Wêi: Ho-nan Province

Wêi-ch'êng: near Ch'ang-an (Hsi-an-fu), in Shen-si Province

Wêi River: in Shen-si Province

West Fort Mountain (Hsi-sai): near Wu-ch'ang, in Hu-pêi Province

Wheel Tower (Lun-t'ai): in Manchuria

White Gate City: Nan-king

White God City (Po-ti): in Sze-chuan Province

White Wolf River (Pai-lang-ho): in Manchuria

Wu: Kiang-su Province

Wu-ch'ang (O-chou): a district by the Han River, now the capital of Hu-pêi Province

Wu-chiang: a district in Kiang-su Province

Wu-chou Mountain: in Chê-kiang Province

Wu-chu Tribes: Manchus

Wu-hsing: a district in Chê-kiang Province

Wu-ling: a district and a river in Hu-nan Province

Wu Valley: in Hsia-chou District, Sze-chuan Province

Wang-ch'uan: in Shen-si Province

Yang-chou (Kuang-ling or Wêi-yang or Wu-chêng or Kiang-tu): a district and city in Kiang-su Province

Yang Gate (Yang-kuan): south of the Jade Pass, between China and Turkestan, now in Kan-su Province

Yang-tsze-kiang: the great artery river between north and south China

Yellow Dragon City (Huang-lung): in Manchuria

Yellow River (Huang-ho): the second largest river, in north China

Yen: the part of Chih-li Province centering at Pe-king

Yen-ch'êng: in Ho-nan Province

Yen-jan: the boundary mountain between China and Manchuria

Yen Mountain: near Hsiang-yang, in Hu-pêi Province

Yi-chou: in Sze-chuan Province

Yieh: a district in Ho-nan Province

Yien River: in Chê-kiang Province

Yin Mountains: between Turkestan and Mongolia

Ying-mên Mountain: in Hu-pêi Province

Yo-chou (Yüeh-yang or Yüeh-chou or Pa-ling): a district in Hu-nan Province

Yu: Chih-li Province

Yü-ch'ien: in Chê-kiang Province

Yu-chou: in Chih-li Province

Yüeh: Chê-kiang Province

Yun Valley: in Hu-pêi Province

Yung: a district in Hu-nan Province

Yun-yang (now San-yuan): a district in Shen-si Province

Yü-yang (now Chi-hsien): a district in Chih-li Province

Yü-yi: a district in An-huêi Province

NOTES ON THE POEMS

1. *The Day of No Fire*. (The Chinese title is *Lines*.) Chieh Chih-t'uêi, a scholar and statesman of the Chin State toward the end of the Chou Dynasty, was disliked by the Duke Wên and exiled to the mountains. Later, trying to find him, but failing, the Duke had the forest set on fire to force him out, and Chieh Chih-t'uêi was burned to death. The Duke, remorseful, ordered the people to mourn the dead man and always to commemorate him on this day, late in spring, by lighting no fires and eating only cold food. When the custom of the Day of No Fire had become fixed, fire of any sort was forbidden until night, and, as told in Han Hung's *After the Day of No Fire,* the Emperor would then send candles to his favourite officials, no others to be lighted before theirs.

1a. The ancient Emperor Wang, who had lost his kingdom, in what is now Sze-chuan, entered at his death into a cuckoo, and his imperial spirit has cried for ever: " Oh, to go back again! " The name " Emperor Wang," meaning " Emperor of Hope," came to be one of the names of the cuckoo. There is a direct allusion to this legend in Li Shang-yin's *The Inlaid Harp.*

2. In an old story by T'ao Ch'ien (A.D. 365–427), the Peach-Blossom River flows to the Utopian land, T'ao-yüan. It seems that long ago a fisherman from Wu-ling, fishing on the river, lost his

way, and, leaving his boat and walking along the bank, found at
its end a little cave. At first narrow and dark, the cave opened
presently into a wide and beautiful place where there were many
people in the streets, dressed in strange fashion. They asked the
fisherman whence he came; but they knew nothing of his country
and age; for their ancestors, so they told him, had fled from the
disorders of the Ch'in Dynasty eight hundred years before and
had never gone back again. They spoke an old tongue and read
old books. They had no laws, they paid no taxes. Everyone worked
his own land and was happy in his own home. Family after family
welcomed the fisherman and invited him to remain among them;
but he thought instead that he would come back later and so said
good-bye to them. He passed through the cave, fixing the way well
in his mind; he returned home and reported his experience. But
when officials of the Government asked him to guide them to
T'ao-yüan, he could never find it again. (See Wang Wêi's *A Song
of the Peach-Blossom River* for a poetic version of the narrative;
see also P'ai Ti's *A Farewell to Ts'uêi*.)

2a. T'ao Ch'ien, the poet who first set down the story, had been
a magistrate at Pêng-tsê and, like Vice-Prefect Liu, to whom
Ts'uêi Shu addresses *A Climb on the Mountain Holiday*, an ap-
preciator of wine and chrysanthemums. Wang Wêi, in *A Message
from my Lodge*, compares P'ai Ti to him by a reference to T'ao
Ch'ien's home, Five Willows.

3. *She Sings an Old Song.* (The Chinese title is *Ho-man-tzŭ*, the
name of the old Song.) According to Po Chü-yi, there was a
singer of Ts'ang-chou in the K'ai-yuan period who, condemned

to die, asked at the last moment to be allowed to sing this song, vainly hoping that it might win him clemency. His name became attached to the song. And it is known that later, in the Emperor Wên-tsung's time, Shên A-ch'iao, a palace-girl, was famous for singing it and dancing to it.

4. Lady Yang Kuêi-fêi, called in the original text of Chang Hu's poem *On the Terrace of Assembled Angels* T'ai-chên (The Ever-True), was the T'ang Emperor Hsüan-tsung's famous favourite. The Ladies Kuo Kuo and Ch'in Kuo were her beautiful sisters. The Premier, mentioned with them in Tu Fu's *A Song of Fair Ladies,* was Yang Kuo-chung, avowedly their brother, but supposed to be even more tenderly interested in them, and likely, therefore, to resent their receiving bluebird messages (love-letters) from other admirers.

4a. As told in Po Chü-yi's *A Song of Unending Sorrow,* Emperor Hsüan-tsung, known also as Ming Huang (Magnificent Monarch), was so enamoured of Lady Yang that he neglected his empire. His vassals revolted, and his armies refused to take orders. Forced to flee the capital, he escaped toward Sze-chuan with his lady and his officials, but even then his own body-guard protested that unless he gave her up, they would desert him. Finally they seized and slew her and officially announced that it had been by his own orders, whereupon the soldiers once more pledged loyalty to the dynasty. In Chêng T'ien's *On Ma-wêi* Slope it is told that they persuaded the Emperor to yield his lady by reminding him of the tragic fate of an earlier monarch, known as " The Later King of the Ch'ên Dynasty." This King also had become unpopular because of

a favourite. He had refused to give her up, and when trouble fol-
lowed, had tied her to himself and hidden in a dry well at Ching-
yang Palace. The revolutionists had found them there and killed
them. Further reference is made to this earlier Emperor, and to
A Song of Courtyard Flowers, which he composed for his favourite,
in Tu Mu's *A Mooring on the Ch'in-huai River* and Li Shang-yin's
The Palace of the Suêi Emperor. Girls on the river at Nan-king
are still singing the song in flower-boats and taverns.

This Emperor was overthrown by the Suêi Emperor, Yang-ti,
who became the most luxurious and depraved of the Chinese
emperors and exhausted the country for his indulgences. In winter,
for the trees of his garden, he had leaves and flowers made of silk,
and birds were slaughtered broadcast that the palace cushions
might be soft with only the finest down. (See Li Shang-yin's *The
Suêi Palace.*) The end of the Suêi Dynasty came with his over-
throw by the founder of the T'ang Dynasty, called "Peak of the
Sun" (Jih-chüeh). Wang Wêi, in the last line of *Looking
Down in a Spring Rain* contrasts a good emperor with Emperor
Yang-ti.

4b. Among the incidents told of Emperor Hsüan-tsung is the
famous occasion when Li Po was called upon by the Emperor to
compose a poem for Lady Yang. It was at the Feast of Peonies,
and the Emperor announced to the poet that he and his guests
wished to hear, not the old poems, but a new one. Happily
drunken, the poet thereupon wrote the three stanzas called *A Song
of Pure Happiness.* They were sung at once, the Emperor himself
playing the melody upon a jade lute. Another lyrical event
is referred to in Po Chü-yi's *A Song of Unending Sorrow.* The

Emperor Hsüan-tsung visited the moon in a dream and was taught there by Chang-o, the Goddess of the Moon, a dance-play called *The Rainbow Skirt and the Feathered Coat.* When he awoke, he remembered it, and, summoning his musicians and actors, the Pear-Garden Players, instructed them in the music and the steps. His beloved Lady Yang performed in the dance. (See note 42.)

4c. There is in this collection one poem by the Emperor himself, *I Pass through Lu Dukedom with a Sigh and a Sacrifice for Confucius,* in which, remembering the dream that brought Confucius an omen of death, the Emperor wonders if he should feel a similar premonition as to his own fate.

4d. Tu Fu, in *A Song of Sobbing by the River,* laments the passing of the Emperor and of Lady Yang. The end of Hsüan-tsung's reign came about in the following manner: An Lu-shan, son of a defeated Hun chieftain, had been captured in his youth, favoured by Hsüan-tsung, and adopted by Lady Yang; but, exiled later because of sedition, he aroused his people and led his bandit troops to the capture of the capital, Ch'ang-an. This was what caused the Emperor's unhappy flight, during which Lady Yang was killed. After An Lu-shan had reigned for a few months, he was murdered by his own adopted son, a Chinese; whereupon Ch'ang-an was recaptured by Chinese troops, and Su-tsung, son of Hsüan-tsung, was made Emperor. That this prince too had his troubles is told in Tu Fu's *A Song of a Prince Deposed.* Tu Fu, although loyal to the dynasty, tells in his poems *A Song of Sobbing* and *Taking Leave of Friends* how, during the troubles, he had fled the capital and was subsequently transferred in punishment to a provincial post.

Yüan Chên, in his poem *The Summer Palace,* speaks of court-ladies, long after Hsüan-tsung's downfall, remembering the brilliant and prosperous thirty years of his reign, before the final ten years of infatuation with Lady Yang, which brought about his ruin.

5. It is believed that this Japanese priest may have been Kobo-daishi, who spent twenty years in China at Ch'ang-an University. Chinese was the only language in which was written the whole Buddhist teaching, the light of which was the "single lantern." Kobo-daishi, returning home, founded the great monastery on Koya-san and devised from Chinese characters the Japanese alphabet, Kana.

"The source" meant China, the super-land in relation to Japan.

5a. The chant is specified in the original as Fan, chanting in Sanskrit; the faith, as in the seventh line of Liu Chang-ch'ing's *While Visiting the Taoist Priest Ch'ang on the South Stream* is the Ch'an doctrine. This Buddhistic doctrine of serenity brought by Ta-mo, or Buddhidharma, from India during the period of the Six Dynasties, and later blent with Taoism, was the Shingon Buddhism carried back by Kobo-daishi to Japan, where it persists today, blent with Zen Buddhism, its principal seat still being the Monastery of Koya-san.

6. The term "The Sun," or "The Light of Heaven," is often used to mean the Emperor, as well as "The Son of Heaven" and "The Ruler of Heaven."

7. The Woman-Emperor Wu-chao (690–704) had established verse-writing as one of the requirements in the Government Examinations, through which, as through western Civil Service, posts of state were conferred. This applicant, having failed to qualify with his verse, feels himself unworthy of the hairpin of his family rank.

7a. Commentators explain that on the eve of his final examination the subject of the poem by Chu Ch'ing-yü, possibly the poet, hopefully addresses a friend who has received the degree and is an expert in the subject. Elaborated metaphor of this kind, rare in the best poetry of the T'ang period, became popular with later poets.

8. The phrase " Jade Dressing-Table " indicates a certain style of poem dealing with women.

The characters for this particular beetle and for good fortune have the same pronunciation, just as have the characters for bat and prosperity or the characters for deer and official Emolument.

The English term, " yoke," is used here as an inadequate equivalent of the original term, " washing-stone," which, though a familiar Chinese word for husband, would not be clear to a western reader.

9. In the Ch'u Kingdom of the Chou Dynasty there were many poets. One of them once wrote a poem and asked the others to " harmonize " it, which they did. Then he wrote another, to which the responses were fewer because it was more difficult. Then he followed with *The Song of Bright Spring*, which only two or three

could harmonize. The title has come to mean a song of the highest order.

There are four ways of harmonizing a poem: to sing of the same subject with any rhymes; with the same rhyme-sound, but different words; with the same rhyme-words, but in a different order; or with the same rhyme-words and in the same order.

9a. Chia Chih had written a poem on the Palace of Light and asked his friends to "harmonize" it. (See the poems called *An Early Audience at the Palace of Light* by Ts'ên Ts'an and Wang Wêi.)

10. The sound of mallets on stone came from women washing goods to make winter clothes, according to the custom still followed in China.

11. "The Purple Hills" was a name for paradise.

12. "Dragon-beard" was a kind of finely woven bamboo matting.

13. Han Yü, for opposing Buddhism, was exiled by Emperor Hsien-tsung. The Emperor had sent envoys to India to import Buddhistic doctrines and was preparing a great ceremony to receive a relic, a bone of the Buddha, when Han Yü, protesting against the introduction of a religion unsuited to China, remarked that whatever virtue there had been in Buddha, there could be none in his bone; which, besides, might be really that of a dog or a sheep. The Emperor angrily exiled the protestant.

On another occasion Han Yü, secretary to the Emperor's Premier, P'ai Tu, wrote an account of the conquering of the Huai-hsi rebels (see Li Shang-yin's *The Han Monument*). This writing was inscribed on stone as a monument of the victory; but afterward, owing to personal jealousy, the monument was cast down and an inferior inscription set in its place. (See Tu Fu's *A Letter to Censor Han*.)

13a. Divinity-cups are still used at temples for telling fortunes. Two small cups, originally of jade, now of wood, are thrown on the ground. The inquirer, kneeling before the altar, is told his lot according to their position and aspect.

14. There are five sacred peaks in China. Hêng-shan, the Nan-yüeh, near Hêng-chou in Hu-nan Province (see Han-yü's *Stopping at a Temple on Hêng Mountain*), is the southernmost of them. Hua-shan, or Tai-hua (the Great Flower), the Hsi-yüeh (see Hsü Hun's *Inscribed in the Inn at T'ung Gate* and Ts'uêi Hao's *Passing through Hua-yin*), is in Shen-si Province and is the westernmost. To westerners the best-known of these mountains is the easternmost, Tai-shan (the Great Peak), the Tung-yüeh near T'ai-an in Shan-tung Province (see Tu Fu's *A View of Tai-shan*). The other two of the sacred peaks are Sung-shan, the Chung-yüeh, the midmost of them, near Lo-yang in Ho-nan Province; and a second Hêng-shan, the Pei-yüeh, the northernmost, near Hun-yuan in Shan-si Province.

On these five mountains (see Han-yü's *Stopping at a Temple*), were conferred titles ranking with those of the Three Dukes, the highest in the Empire.

14a. The Purple Canopy, Celestial Column, Stone Granary, and Fire God, are four mountain peaks around Hêng-shan, the Holy Mountain in Hu-nan Province.

15. Among the oldest known stone-carvings of the Chinese, these ten stone drums were made and engraved with poems, under the Emperor Hsüan of the Chou Dynasty. Three of them still exist and are now in the Confucian Temple at Peking, together with replicas of the other seven.

16. The writings of Wang Hsi-chih, even in his own time, were very valuable; but he would not sell them, except in exchange for a few white geese, of which he was extremely fond.

17. There is a popular anonymous parody of this poem, made by changing only two or three characters, mocking a husband who on a trip to the city had abandoned his moustache:

I left home old. I return young,
Speaking as then, but with no hair on my lip;
And my goodwife, meeting me, does not know me.
She smiles and says: " Little boy, where do you come from? "

18. The last two lines are reminiscent of a poem by Sung Yü of the Chou Dynasty (300 B.C.) which concludes:

A single leaf, blown from a lakka-tree,
Whispers autumn through the world.

19. Tsou was a dukedom within the Lu Realm, in what is now Shan-tung.

During the Han Dynasty the Lu Duke, breaking down the walls of his palace and finding ancient writings, recognized it as the former abode of Confucius and therefore transformed it into a temple.

19a. In the *Analects* Confucius said: " When the phœnix no longer comes, it will mean the end of my fortunes." When a dead *ch'i-lin,* akin to a unicorn, was brought to him by official hunters for identification, he recognized it as the creature which was wont to appear for greeting during a successful reign, but he grieved that this time its coming had meant its death. He wrote a poem to it:

> Unicorn and phœnix came once to happy kings.
> What made you come at the wrong time, only to die?
> Unicorn, unicorn, my heart is full of pity.

A few days before he died, he told his disciples that he had fore-seen his end in a dream, in which he had found himself at a large temple, witness of a sacrificial ceremony being conducted between two pillars, and he wrote this poem about it:

> Alas, is this the crumbling of T'ai-shan?
> Alas, is this the rotting of the beam?
> Alas, is this the wise man's withering?

20. She weaves like the Lady Su Huêi, who embroidered the famous eight-hundred-character anagram, from which have been discovered already, as told in Dr. Kiang's Introduction, several hundred rhyming poems.

21. Wu Valley in the Hsia-chung district, Sze-chuan Province, is the destination of one friend; and Hêng Mountain near Ch'angsha, in Hu-nan Province, is the destination of the other.

"Dew from Heaven," in the original text, refers to the Emperor's favour.

22. The Yen Song was a musical song of the northern border.

The Great Chief, Chan-yü, was the title of the King of the Tartars who invaded China.

Li Mu, of the Chao State in Chou Dynasty, had killed more than ten thousand Tartars, so that for a decade after there had been no more invaders.

23. Ts'ai Yen, called also Ts'ai Wên-chi, daughter of a famous scholar of the later Han Dynasty, was captured by Tartars and made the wife of their chieftain. She expressed her grief in a melody of eighteen stanzas on a barbarian musical instrument, *hu-chia.*

Musical notes in China still have the old names. The *shang,* the *chüeh,* and the *yü* are the second, third, and fifth of the total five.

24. Emperor Wu of the Han Dynasty, for the purpose of introducing grape-vines into China, had tried to conquer central Asia.

25. The Chinese or Han Princess, Wang Ch'ao-chün, the Lady of Light, was a beautiful court-lady living at the palace of Emperor Ch'êng. Since there were too many girls there for the Emperor to select from except by portrait, Mao Yen-shou made all their

likenesses, painting them favourably or unfavourably according to the size of their bribes. The Lady Wang, failing to bribe, was made to look unsightly. And, when a chieftain of the Huns sent envoys to the Emperor, offering to submit to the Han Dynasty if he might marry into the imperial family, the Emperor chose, among those whom he did not desire, Wang Ch'ao-chün and sent her word asking whether she would like to go. She agreed; preferring, say some, to be the wife of the Hun rather than obscure in the Han palace. At the farewell feast Emperor Ch'êng found her, unlike her portrait, very beautiful. But it was too late; he had given his word to the envoys. So she married the Hun chieftain. When she died, she was buried, as she had requested, alongside the Chinese boundary, close to the Great Wall. And where she lies, the grass, which everywhere else on the Hun side is yellow, is as green as it is on the Chinese side. Po Chü-yi has a poem on *The Exiled Lady Wang Ch'ao-chün*:

> Let the envoy, going back to China, say this:
> Her heart is timing the day of return,
> And yet, should the Emperor wish to be told,
> This foreign sunlight is good for her beauty.

A play about her by Wang Shih-fu has been translated into English by Sir John Davis under the title *The Sorrow of Han*.

Lady Wang wrote the words and music of an eighteen-stanza song and used to play it on her guitar (*p'i-p'a*). When in Chinese paintings a woman is seen playing a guitar on horseback, it is she.

See Tu Fu's *Thoughts of Old Time*. In this volume it consists of only two of five poems he wrote under the one title, which is, more literally, *Pondering on Old Ruins*.

26. Wu Mountain was the abode of nymphs and fairies. It is told
that a supernally beautiful fairy appeared once in a dream to King
Hsiang of Ch'u, and to his entreaties answered only that she was
" morning-cloud and evening-rain upon the hills of Wu." " Cloud
and rain " has come to be in Chinese a phrase indicating passionate
love.

26a. Flying Swallow, Chao Fêi-yen, originally a singing-girl and
a famous beauty, became a favourite of Emperor Ch'êng of the
Han Dynasty, in the first century B.C. As remembered in Tu Mu's
Confession, this lady was supposed to be so exquisitely slender
that she could dance on the palm of the hand.

27. Mr. Ezra Pound in his *Cathay,* translating this and other
poems by Li Po, misled readers for a period by using the Japanese
name Rihoku. The reason for this would appear to be that Mr.
Pound discovered the poems among the papers of Fenellosa and,
finding the name as set down by some Japanese scholar, did not
recognize the poet as the great Li Po. Other translators have used
the name Li T'ai-po. Li was his family name, Po his given name,
and T'ai-po his social name.

28. Yang-chou, called in Li Po's poem Kuang-ling, at the southern
end of the Grand Canal, was in T'ang times a rich and luxurious
city, of which it was said:

> Happy is he who has a million
> And can ride on the stork back to Yang-chou.

It was a gala resort for the wealthy and distinguished.

28a. The Yellow Crane Terrace was a famous building on a terrace by the Yang-tsze at Wu-chang, Hu-pêi Province. (The Chinese word for it means literally a building of more than one story, a word for which we do not find an equivalent in English.)

Wang Tzŭ-ch'iao, attaining immortality six hundred years before Christ, is said to have flown up to heaven at this spot on the back of a yellow crane. The building commemorated the event. Li Po once came to it and wished to inscribe a poem, but finding Ts'uêi Hao's poem on the wall, wrote the following lines:

> Let my fist break down the Yellow Crane Terrace
> And my foot kick over Parrot Isle,
> Whose loveliness but finds me dumb —
> With Ts'uêi Hao's poem above my head.

29. This poem is an example of what the Chinese call one-current-of-air poetry, *yi-ch'i-ho-ch'êng*.

30. General Hsieh Shang of the Chin Dynasty was Commander of the Guard in the region about Niu-chu. He was also a literary man and a poet. One moonlight evening he heard somebody reading poetry in a small boat. On inquiry, he found that it was Yüan Hung, a very young poet, reading from his own works. The general sent for him and praised him highly. Yüan Hung afterwards became well known. Near here, according to some of his friends, Li Po was drowned while trying to embrace a reflection of the moon; and it is possible that this was his last poem.

31. The poet had evidently been sent away from Ch'ang-an, the capital.

32. Li po, as well as Wang Wêi, Mêng Hao-jan, Tsu Yung, and others of the T'ang poets, seems to have enjoyed the region around Chung-nan Mountain, fifteen miles south of the capital, Ch'ang-an, in Shen-si Province.

32a. The Emperor, upon reading Mêng's poem about Chung-nan, was indignant and declared that the famous poet had not been dismissed, but, as Li Po declares in *A Message to Mêng Hao-jan,* had left service of his own accord.

33. The post and the tower of silent watching refer to two stories. This is one of the stories. A young man once waited for a girl by a certain post under a bridge. She was delayed. Rather than leave the appointed spot, he clung to the post and was drowned by the rising tide. The girl, arriving late, and seeing the fate of her lover, killed herself. This is the other story. Two young people, deeply in love, were married. After much happiness, the husband felt impelled to become a recluse. Sadly, but resolutely, he went away to a mountain-side and established his retreat. His wife then built a high tower, in the top of which she lived for many long years, her gaze ever fixed towards the mountain and her hermit.

34. The "madman" was Chieh-yü, a Ch'u Kingdom recluse, famous for drinking, but more for stopping Confucius's chariot and warning him against politics with the song:

> O phœnix, O phœnix,
> Virtue is corrupted!
> What is past is past all counsel,

What is future may be moulded, —
But come away, come away,
Politics are dangerous!

Wang Wêi, in the original of the next to the last line of *A Message from my Lodge,* refers to P'ai Ti as Chieh-yü.

The Stone Mirror: a peak near Lu Mountain.

34a. Hsieh Ling-yun: a famous scholar of the Chin Dynasty (see Li Po's *T'ien-mu Mountain*).

" The immortal pellet " was a drug made by Taoist alchemists and supposed to confer immortality. " The lute's third playing " refers to the fact that there were usually three stanzas in a song.

The Jade City: the capital of heaven.

Saint Lu-ao had been mentioned by Chuang-tzŭ as ascending into heaven.

35. This villa at Hsüan-chou, in what is now An-huêi Province, was named after Hsieh T'iao, a famous writer of the Chin Dynasty who was known as the Lesser Hsieh because he was the nephew of the still more famous writer of the same surname, Hsieh Ling-yun, known as the Great Hsieh. Li Po, in high compliment, compares himself to Secretary Shu-yun as the Lesser Hsieh to the Great Hsieh. (See Li Po's *Lu Mountain* and *T'ien Mu Mountain*.)

" The bones of great writers " carries in the original a specific reference to Chien-an, a celebrated period of letters during the Wêi Dynasty of the Three Kingdoms.

36. The road Li Po is describing runs from Shen-si Province (Ch'in) to Sze-chuan Province (Shu). In the original text the two

early rulers are named: Ts'an-tsung and Yü-fu, both of the legendary ages.

"The City of Silk": Chêng-tu, the capital of Sze-chuan Province.

37. She was in Ch'ang-an, the T'ang capital, and he near Yen-jan, a boundary mountain. She has set down her harp from Chao (Chih-li Province) and significantly taken up her Sze-chuan lute, with its strings in attuned pairs.

38. The master, Ts'ên, refers to the poet, Ts'ên Ts'an, and the scholar, Tan Ch'iu, to a Taoist hermit of the early T'ang period, whose real name was unknown.

Prince Ch'ên was Ts'ao Chih of the Wêi Dynasty in the Three Kingdoms period.

The translation "flower-dappled horse" simplifies a comparison in the original to the five-flowered coin, a comparison which, though familiar and quick to the Chinese imagination, would for a Westerner impede the rush of the poem. (See Ts'ên Ts'an *A Song of Running Horse River*.)

39. The poet, according to Chinese custom means himself when in the original he names someone well known to whose lot or experience his own may be likened. Ssŭ-ma Hsiang-ju of the Han Dynasty, a famous scholar, was the guest of Prince Liang, but later retired and died in Mao-ling. The story is told that, invited to the house of a rich man, Cho Wang-sun, Hsiang-ju with a lute sang so beautifully his poem, *The Phœnix in Search of his Mate*, that Wên-chün, Cho Wang-sun's nineteen-year-old widowed daughter, fell in love with him. Rapt in wine, he sang with his

lute another song, asking her to elope. She did. Having no money, they opened and conducted a small wine-house; and though the father, through family pride, bade them come home, the poet refused. The resort was so obscure that the Emperor Ch-êng, who liked his poetry, could not find him. But the Empress, unloved, discovered him and persuaded him with a bribe to write a poem with which she could regain imperial favour. This poem, which was read to the Emperor as hers, causing him to love her again, is a long one and still extant.

39a. Carp in the river and wildgeese or bluebirds in the sky were the classical messengers of love, or of friendship. In one of the Nineteen Ancient Poems, the poet tells how he was brought some carp by a boy and, cutting one of them open, found in its belly a letter from his beloved, declaring her love and wishing him happiness.

40. Only officials above the third rank in the T'ang Dynasty wore the decoration of the Golden Tortoise.

41. It was believed that paradise, with its Jade Pool, lay to the west of China and that there stood also the palace of Hsi-wang-mu, the Royal Mother of the West. Stories are frequent, in Chinese and Japanese literature and art, of emperors trying to communicate with her kingdom. Emperor Mu of the Chou Dynasty had eight horses, able to cover ten thousand miles in a day. Driving them west, he reached the kingdom and found the goddess. But he never returned. And *The Yellow Bamboo Song* was composed as a mourning-song for him and his followers, all but a few of whom died on the way.

42. In ancient stories, King Yi was cruel to his wife, Ch'ang-o. Planning to escape him, she stole from heaven a miraculous potion by means of which she might flee away and be safe. When she had drunk the potion, she began to run very fast and could not stop. Finally she entered the moon and was unable to find her way out. So she remained there and became its goddess, her husband becoming, in his turn, God of the Sun. (See notes 4b and 91.)

43. When only twenty-four years old, Chia Yi, a statesman and man of letters, sent a ten-thousand-word memorial, offering his political views and plans for reform, to Emperor Wên of the Han Dynasty. The period was prosperous and the Emperor, though not warm-hearted, was a just ruler. But Chia Yi was sensitive and had fears for the future. Everyone thought him crazy. Even the Emperor considered him a visionary whose dreams were of no value, and sent him as a petty official to Ch'ang-sha, now capital of Hu-nan Province, but at that time an out-of-the-way place, where he died. After thirty or forty years his prophecies came true and he was remembered. While at Ch'ang-sha, he acted as tutor to a prince, as mentioned in Liu Chang-ch'ing's *New Year's*. Near the Hsiang River, Chia Yi had written a poem eulogizing Chü Yuan, the famous poet, who in exile had drowned himself there. In the same locality Liu Chang-ch'ing, also in exile, wrote *On Passing Chia Yi's House in Ch'ang-sha*. The same poet's *A Poem Sent to Governor Yuan* intimates that Liu Chang-ch'ing in exile was as meritorious as Chia Yi.

44. It was a poetical belief that the cicada was the purest member of the insect world and lived only upon dew. Its advice to Li

Shang-yin is rather to die nobly of hunger at home with his family than to lead an ignoble and uncertain official life.

45. *The Precious Dagger* was a long poem by Kuo Yüan-chên sent to the T'ang Woman-Emperor, Wu-Chao. (See note 7.) The theme of the poem was that a good scholar is like a precious dagger. The poet was summoned to become her attendant. During the fifty years of her successful reign, akin in more ways than one to the reign of Queen Elizabeth in England, Tibet was conquered, and part of Turkestan.

45a. The Blue Houses are the quarters of the dancing-girls.

46. Chuang-tzǔ, dreaming once that he had been transformed into a butterfly, awoke to find the butterfly gone and his own body on the bed. He said: "I do not know which is my real self, this or the butterfly." Another story is told of him. Walking with his friend Huêi-tzǔ, he saw some fish in the water and said: "How happy they are!" Huêi answered: "You are not a fish; how do you know they are happy?" And Chüang retorted: "You are not I. How do you know I do not know that they are happy?"

The tears of merfolk were supposed to become pearls. It was believed that in the fields of paradise grew only jewels and jade, which, under the sun's heat, would give off their colours in mist.

47. *Nameless Lines* are always love-poems, the designation having become a custom. We translate the title *To One Unnamed*.

48. In the original seventh line, Liu is named in the poet's place. Liu went once to a mountain, met a nymph there, and was enter-

tained; but, coming away, lost his direction and never found it again; like the famous fisherman from Wu-ling, who lost his way to the Peach-Blossom Country.

It was supposed that a lock decorated with a golden toad was thereby made secure.

The jade tiger was a marker on a well-rope, gauging the water's depth.

Lady Chia, the daughter of a premier of the Chin Dynasty, and specified in the original text, fell in love with her father's young secretary, Han Shou, and finally married him, in spite of his low rank. Her father, recognizing on Han Shou's clothes a particular scent used by his daughter, could not withhold his approval of the marriage.

Prince Wêi, also specified in the original, met on the Lo River a fairy, Lady Mi, who gave him a bridal mat and disappeared. He wrote about the episode, a long and beautiful account in rhythmic prose.

49. General Chu-kê Liang, called also K'ung-ming, is a familiar figure in these poems. He was a celebrated general, scholar and statesman in the period of the Three Kingdoms, who as Premier advised and served the founder of the Shu Kingdom, Emperor Liu Pêi, restored rebellious lands, and in later times was honoured and worshipped by the people. (See Tu Fu's *A Song of an Old Cypress, The Temple of the Premier of Shu,* and *Thoughts of Old Time, II.*)

49a. The Eight-Sided Fortress (*pa-chên-t'u*) was built on Chu-kê Liang's plan of the eight diagrams, beside the Upper Yang-tsze in Sze-chuan. He advised his Emperor, campaigning against the other two kingdoms, to master the Wêi Kingdom first; but the Emperor, rejecting his advice, attacked first the Wu Kingdom and was defeated. (See note 52a.)

49b. Emperor Liu Pêi, before his accession, went twice to Chu-kê Liang's hut for counsel and was refused; but the third time, when the Emperor knelt by the bed and said: "Not for my sake, but for the sake of my people, assist me," Chu-kê Liang consented. He remained Premier into the reign of the succeeding Emperor. Finally, as general, he planned a victory which his death prevented.

Historians regard Emperor Liu Pêi, founder of the Shu Kingdom, as carrying on the Han Dynasty against two usurpers in the other two of the Three Kingdoms, Shu, Wu, and Wêi, which in Liu Yu-hsi's poem *The Temple of the First King of Shu* are likened to a three-legged pot. The same poem refers to the fact that in the other kingdoms the five-pennyweight coin was given less than its proper weight. The "great premier" in this poem was the famous Chu-kê Liang.

49c. The Later Emperor of the Shu Kingdom, the second whom Chu-kê Liang served and advised, was defeated and captured after the Premier's death.

The Liang-fu Song (Song of the Holy Mountain) concerning one of the peaks of Tai-shan, had been written by Chu-kê Liang while he was still a hermit, and before he yielded to the Emperor's third request for assistance.

49d. In Tu Fu's *Night in the Watch-Tower,* Chu-kê Liang is referred to as "Sleeping Dragon," and Kung-sun Shu, another Han general, as "Plunging Horse."

50. Kuan and Yüeh, specified in the original, were statesmen of
the Chou Dynasty. Kuan and Chang, also specified, two great
generals in the Shu Kingdom, were both killed in action; the first
of them, Kuan Yü, has been made the Chinese god of war, called
also Kuan Ti.

51. The *Canons of Yao and Hsun* were two volumes in the Con-
fucian Book of History, *Ch'ing-miao* and *Shêng-min* two poems
in the Confucian Book of Poetry, and the T'ang plate and Con-
fucian tripod two art treasures.

    The three Huang rulers and five Ti rulers were famous as
good sovereigns of ancient China.

52. Chou Yü, a hero of the period of the Three Kingdoms, young,
handsome, a statesman, a general, a scholar, a musician, was fond
of listening to classical music and when a mistake would be made
is said to have reminded the player with a glance. The listener here
is of course not Chou Yü, but one whose eye the harpist likes to
attract, and probably also a connoisseur of music.

52a. In Tu Mu's *The Purple Cliff* (a cliff on the Yang-tsze, east
of Han-kou, Hu-pêi Province) allusion is made to a celebrated
event occurring there, an exploit of Chou Yü's. A fleet from the
Wêi Kingdom had come down the river to attack the Wu and
Shu Kingdoms. The two generals, Chu-kê Liang of the Shu
Kingdom, and Chou Yü of the Wu Kingdom, combined forces
and destroyed the fleet by setting it afire. The King of Wêi, if
he had won this battle, would have been able to bear captive to his
Copper-Bird Palace the two famously beautiful girls of Ch'iao,

one of them the wife of the King of Wu and the other the wife of General Chou Yü. These girls are celebrated in Chinese poetry, like Helen of Troy in European poetry, as a romantic source of war. In Tu Fu's poem *The Eight-Sided Fortress,* is sung Chu-kê Liang's grief that he had not conquered the Wu Kingdom; yet here are seen the Wu and Shu Kingdoms allied against the Wêi Kingdom. Changes in the military alignment of Chinese war-lords have always been rapid.

53. This temple, in Yang-chou, Kiang-su Province, was on a ter-race erected by General Wu of the Ch'ên Dynasty and was named after him.

The river is the Yang-tsze.

54. In the original text of Liu Chang-ch'ing's *On Leaving Kiu-kiang* the familiar poetical term " Green-Wave Islands " is used for Ch'ang-an, the capital, from which he had been previously exiled because of a storm he had aroused by too freely expressing his own ideas.

In the original of Shên Ch'üan-ch'i's *Beyond Seeing,* the capi-tal, is called " The City of the Red Phœnix "; and in Wang Wêi's *To Chi-wu Ch'ien,* " The Gate of Gold."

55. The fellow-official sent to Lien-chou was Liu Yü-hsi, the poet.

56. The clans of Wang and Shieh, specified in the original, had been prominent in Nan-king. They had lived on Blacktail Row, which, decaying in the superseded capital, was now left to the swallows and the poor.

57. In the period of the Three Kingdoms, the Yang-tsze River was fortified with chains to defend Nan-king, capital of the Wu Kingdom. But Wang Chün, of the Chin Dynasty, building high-storied war-ships, brought them down from Sze-chuan, managed to cut to pieces the iron chains at the mouth of the river, and so captured the city.

58. The original text of the second line reads: "Sings me what I am thinking under my southern cap." A prisoner from the south would wear all of the northern prison-garb, but keep his own cap to remember his own land. And the phrase "southern cap" has come to symbolize a political prisoner, with the implication that he maintains his ideas. This prisoner, for instance, cannot make his pure thoughts heard by the Emperor through the noise of the confused world.

59. Li Kuang of the Han Dynasty, an eminent general against the Tartars, shot one night at a black tiger and next morning found that the point of his arrow was stuck in a solid piece of rock. There is brief reference to him in Wang Wêi's *Song of an Old General*. In Wang Ch'ang-ling's *Over the Border* he is called "The Winged General." (See note 111.)

60. There was a myth that when the two sisters, O-huang and Nü-yin, wives of the dead Emperor Shun, had finished their period of mourning, they became Queens of the Clouds. Lake Tung-t'ing is the only place from which comes a certain spotted bamboo popular with both Chinese and Japanese for its decorative effect. The spots were made by the Queens' tears.

61. Yang Hu of the Chin Dynasty, a governor stationed at Hsiang-yang, now in Hu-pêi Province, was famous as scholar, statesman and general and was much loved by the people. After his death a monument was erected on the Yen Mountain and inscribed with his deeds and was visited by so many mourners that it was called the Monument of Tears.

62. The bluebird, a messenger of the affections, summoned him to the house of his friend, whom he likens to the Han Dynasty Genie of the Red Pine. (See note 89.)

62a. Taoists were often alchemists, with crucibles and potions. Wêi Ying-wu in his *Poem to a Taoist Hermit* speaks of his friend "boiling white stones" — to be eaten thereafter like potatoes.

63. The original second line reads: "If I had enough for the Three Paths." The Three Paths indicated a hermit's hut, one to the front door, one to the back door, and one around the house.

In ancient alchemy it was believed that the flame of cinnamon-wood consumed gold.

64. In Mêng Hao-jan's poem the phrase used for the Mountain Holiday, a day on which everyone goes mountain-climbing for seeing the view, drinking wine, and writing poems, is the Feast of the Two Nines, the ninth day of the ninth month. In Wang Wêi's *On the Mountain Holiday* reference is made to the custom of each climber's carrying a spray of dogwood. Ts'uêi Shu also has a poem concerning this festival.

65. The ancient hermitage is specified as that of P'ang, a hermit who lived on Lu-mên Mountain during the Han Dynasty; but the hermitage meant is probably Mêng's own.

66. The Great Dipper is compared to Kê-shu, the famous T'ang general who conquered Tibet, between which and China ran the Ling-t'ao River.

67. One of the palace luxuries was a pillow under which charcoal and incense were arranged, for fragrant warmth.

68. Wang Sun, a name akin to the English "Prince Charming," but more serious, and translated here "Prince of Friends," means a noble-hearted young scholar or, sometimes, lover. (See Wang Wêi's *A Parting* and *An Autumn Evening in the Mountains*.)
There was an old song:

> The wild grass loves Wang Sun
> And he the grasses;
> And when he rides away,
> They call to him.

69. The places mentioned in Po Chü-yi's note were widely separate: in Shan-si, Ho-nan, An-huêi, and Kiang-si Provinces.

70. Li Yen-nien of the Han Dynasty had said of an earlier beauty than Yang Kuêi-fêi:

> One glance, and she could shatter down a city;
> A second, she could tip an empire over.

71. The instrument translated "guitar" was a *p'i-p'a*, like the Japanese *biwa*, as in Tu Fu's *Thoughts of Old Time, I*. (See note 25.)

72. Sêng, the poet's name, is a variant of Sanka, given as a family name to Buddhist priests.

73. Between Kiang-si and Kuang-tung, even the wildgeese find the Ta-yü (Great Granary) Mountains too high to cross.

Plum-blossoms have not yet opened farther north; but there are plenty in the warm south beyond this mountain.

74. The morning bell, tokening here the separation of friends, was a popular subject among poets as a symbol of finality. For instance, the Chinese spring, beginning on the first day of the First-month, corresponding to early February, ends on the thirtieth day of the Third-month, in our May; and its definite close is sung by Chia Tao in the latter two lines of a four-line poem called *The Thirtieth Day of the Third-Month:*

> I shall lie and share with you, awake,
> The last of spring, till the morning bell.

75. "The Way" (Tao) is the Way of the Universe, the Flow of Unison. It is the essence of Taoism.

At the age of thirty-one, when his wife died, Wang Wêi left his post as Assistant-Secretary of State and, as told in his poem *My Retreat at Chung-nan*, came to live by Mount Chung-nan, turning his heart to the teachings of Lao-tzŭ.

75a. Lao-tzŭ, the founder and teacher of Taoism, despairing of mankind's acceptance of the Way, rode westward on a dun-coloured cow and disappeared for ever in the desert wilderness. At the wall, however, the guard of the gate, of whom nothing is known but his name, Yin-hsi, stopped the aged saint and kept him overnight at the border to set down his principles. The result was the famous mystical book *Tao-tê-ching:* Tao being the "Way" and Tê the exemplification of the mystical philosophy. (See Ts'uêi-shu's *A Climb on the Mountain Holiday* and Liu Chang-ch'ing's *While Visiting a Taoist Priest.*)

76. The Green Books: Chinese official history.

77. The references in the last two lines are to two youths of the Han Dynasty. The first, Pan Ch'ao, in his boyhood a copyist, threw his writing-brush to the ground one day and exclaimed: "I will join the army and fight the Huns!" He became later a famous and successful general. The other, Chung Chün, going to the border to fight the Huns, took off his student cap at the gate and demanded in exchange a lariat, with which he captured Hun chieftains.

78. Emperor Wên of the Han Dynasty, having trouble with the meaning of Lao-tzŭ's book, sent for the Old Magician of the River Bank, of whose wisdom he had heard. The wizard answered: "If the Emperor asked something else, I would go to him. But if he asks the meaning of Tao and Tê, he should come to me." Whereupon the Emperor visited him and referred to the Confucian Book of Poems, in which it says that every being within

the Empire is subject to the emperor. The old man raised himself to the middle of the sky and answered: "Above I do not touch heaven, nor in the centre man, nor below earth. To whom am I subject?" The Emperor bowed and asked him other questions; but the wizard, dropping him a volume, a commentary on the *Tao-tê-ching,* vanished. Later, to commemorate the event, the Emperor built on the spot this Terrace Whence One Sees the Magician (*Wang-Hsien-T'ai*).

79. Tu Ch'iu-niang was a singing-girl, the only woman poet in this anthology.

80. This famous performer, Li Kuêi-nien, was court-musician to Emperor Hsüan-tsung.

81. Ch'ü Yüan, author of *The Songs of Ch'u,* the first rhythmic prose in Chinese, had drowned himself in the Mi-lo River.

82. In the original text, Premier Fang Kuan is indirectly meant by a direct allusion to Premier Hsieh An of the Chin Dynasty, famously fond of chess. Fang is likened also to Lord Hsü, in reference to the following story. Prince Chi-cha of the Chou Dynasty had a very fine dagger, and he knew that Lord Hsü, through whose lands he was passing, coveted it and would not ask for it. The Prince was travelling and could not be without it. When he returned from his journey, Lord Hsü was dead; and Chi-cha, visiting the tomb, hung on a tree there the coveted dagger.

83. Hearing that the bandits have been dispersed in Northern Chi (Chih-li Province), the poet sets out from Chien Station in Sze-chuan, and passing in that province the two mountains, Pa-hsia and Wu-hsia, he reaches Hsiang-yang, in Hu-pêi Province, on his way home to Lo-yang in Ho-nan Province. These names, in the original text, are used in effective succession.

84. For a literal translation of this poem, character by character, see Dr. Kiang's Introduction.

85. Yi and Lü were celebrated early statesmen; and in the following line of the original text, Hsiao and Ts'ao were also specified: the greatest statesmen of the Han Dynasty.

86. Lao-tzŭ had said in the *Tao-tê-ching*: " The heavenly net is broad. It is loose, but never loses."

87. " The late Emperor " was Hsüan-tsung, and the Kuos the family of the famous general Kuo Tzŭ-yi. (See notes 4 and 4a, b, c, d.) T'ai-tsung was the grandfather of Hsüan-tsung.

One of the lines from this poem, " The high clear glance, the deep firm breath," is a phrase frequently quoted as applying to superior literature and brushmanship.

Secretary Wêi Fêng was himself a painter, as of course was Prince Chiang-tu; and Chih Tun was a famous horse-painter of the Chin Dynasty.

88. Lady Wêi was tutor of Wang Hsi-chih, who was a sage of the brush. (See note 16.)

The emperor referred to was Hsüan-tsung.

The origin of the line in which we use the phrase "founders of this dynasty" contains the names of the Princes Pao and Ê, two great generals who helped found the T'ang Dynasty, and in the later line in which we use the phrase "even the finest are deprived of their spirit," the original text specified Hua and Liu, two celebrated horses.

Han Kan's horse-paintings are much admired to this day.

89. "Unicorn" is the best translation we can make of the sacred animal, *ch'i-ling*. (See note 19a.)

The southern rivers are specified in the original as the Hsiao and Hsiang, which are in Hu-nan Province.

Of the Wizard of the Red Pine we have said: "After his earlier follower he has now a new disciple." Tu Fu's text reads: "He has a new disciple, a very Chang Liang." Chang Liang was a great statesman, especially known as a wise adviser to the founder of the Han Dynasty. After Emperor Kao-tzu succeeded in unifying China, Chang Liang retired and followed his Taoist tutor, the Wizard of the Red Pine, and disappeared. Using a common convention in Chinese poetry, Tu Fu names Chang Liang, but means Censor Han, whose merit and case are comparable.

90. This was the temple of Chu-kê Liang. (See notes 49 and 49a, b, c, d.) The temple stood outside the city of Ch'êng-tu, the capital of Sze-chuan.

The poem intimates that in the reconstruction of a country strong statesmen are needed, but that it is difficult to enlist and direct their strength.

91. "Grassy writing" is familiarly and improperly referred to as the running handwriting, the same Chinese character meaning grass and draught.

In Chinese mythology, Yi, the famous archer, shot down from the sky nine of the ten suns and became afterward king of the one sun left; his wife, Chang-o, becoming Queen of the Moon. (See Li Shang-yin's *To the Moon Goddess,* also notes 4b and 42.)

The Pear-Garden Players were the imperial troupe of actors at the court of Emperor Hsüan-tsung. (See note 4b.)

92. The deposed Prince may have been Su-tsung. (See note 4d.)

The crow, especially the white-headed, is a bird of ill omen.

The final line means that the spirits of the five emperors of the T'ang Dynasty are befriending the deposed Prince.

93. The term Spring Palace is still used in China to connote venery.

94. The Chao Tomb, specified in the original, was the tomb of Emperor T'ai-tsung, the second ruler of the T'ang Dynasty, and the most illustrious.

95. In the original, the river region is specified as Chiang-nan, the region along the lower Yang-tsze.

There is still a place in Yang-chou called Twenty-Four Bridges. It probably meant arches.

96. In the original, the two stars are named — the Cowherd and the Spinning-girl (Ch'ien-niu and Chih-nü): the reference being

to a well-known story, the conclusion of which is that two sweet-hearts, having been changed into stars, are able to see each other across the Milky Way, but are allowed to meet only once a year, on the seventh night of the Seventh-month. Lafcadio Hearn has translated from the Japanese a long poem on this subject.

97. The man who owned this garden, Shih Ch'ung of the Chin Dynasty, was the richest man of his time. The last line of this poem alludes to one of many stories about him. A certain general coveted a favourite of his, a girl named Lu-chu, whom Shih Ch'ung refused to surrender. Presently the general, charging him with treason, sent troops to seize Lu-chu. She shut herself in her high chamber; and when they took Shih Ch'ung, she threw herself from the window to her death.

98. It was a poetical belief that the call of the wildgoose came never from pairs, but only from the solitary.

99. Tu Shên-yen was Tu Fu's grandfather.

100. The Court of Perpetual Faith meant the Ladies' Palace, and the Court of the Bright Sun the Emperor's Palace — where apparently some darker lady was in favour.

101. We have translated as "eastern song" the definite phrase of the original, "Yüeh song," meaning a song of Che-kiang Province.

The orchid is known in China as the Flower of the Scholar.

102. The last line probably means that Chinese civilization had not crossed the boundary.

103. Wang Wêi is not only one of China's great poets, but one of her great painters. Su Tung-po of the Sung Dynasty said of him: "In his poems we find his paintings, in his paintings his poems."

104. This song is still popular as a song of farewell, and to this day the expression is often used, "Since we picked willow branches," meaning: "Since we parted."

105. In the original the girls who paid tribute were specified as the Han girls, and the quarrelling farmers as Pa people.

Wên-wêng was a Han Dynasty official, famous as being the first to civilize what is now Sze-chuan Province.

106. From the time of the Han Dynasty, palace guards wore red caps before dawn. The guard of the inner gate would announce dawn, and the others would echo his call till all the gates were opened.

The Jade Cloud Furs, the Pearl Crown, and the Dragon Robe were accoutrements of the Emperor.

During the Han Dynasty there stood in the palace courtyard great bronze giants, holding up their hollowed palms to catch the dew of heaven.

The last line refers to the promulgation of the imperial edict from a five-coloured silken scroll by a procession of officials, one of whom was Chia Chih.

107. It is told by Chuang-tzǔ, that Yang-tzǔ, the scholar, before he became a student of Lao-tzǔ, was highly respected and honoured by his fellow men. Later, through the many years of his discipleship, he lost his prestige, and even a boor would take precedence over him; but he was glad, because he had got rid of pretensions.

There once was a hermit who was fond of sea-gulls; and they followed him wherever he went. His father, asking why they were not frightened, bade the son bring him some. But next day, when the hermit went out intending to take them to his father, they all flew away.

108. *Oh, to go Back Again!* is a song from the Confucian Book of Poems.

109. When the Yüeh Kingdom (now Chê-kiang) was conquered by the Wu Kingdom (now Kiang-su), the Yüeh King still held his throne and plotted to throw off the tributary yoke. Aided by his able minister Fan Li, he planned to distract the King of Wu with women. Fan Li searched through the Yüeh Kingdom for beautiful girls and came upon Hsi Shih washing clothes beside a lake. Controlling his own love for her, he fiercely persuaded her to his plan. She remained at court for some time; and the Wu King, in his infatuation, forgot affairs of state. Weakened by this means, the Wu Kingdom was eventually overcome by the Yüeh Kingdom. Fan Li afterwards refused all reward except Hsi Shih, whom he then took travelling through the Five Lakes, the famous sacred lakes corresponding to the Five Sacred Mountains. There is an allusion to this in Wên T"ing-yun's *Near Li-chou Ferry*.

Hsi Shih suffered from heart-trouble; and men said that her drawn brows, her look of gentleness in suffering, which the girls of her time tried unsuccessfully to imitate, increased her beauty.

110. In the original text where we have used the phrase " the richest men of old," Chi-lun and Shih Ch'ung are specified, celebrated rich men of the Chin Dynasty; and toward the end, where we have used the phrase " hosts of the gayest mansions," the original specifies Chao and Li, well-known rich men of the Han Dynasty who maintained in their homes many dancing-girls.

111. The Horseman of Yieh was Ts'ao Chang, a son of the founder of the Wêi Dynasty in the period of the Three Kingdoms.

General Wêi Ch'ing and General Li Kuang were contemporary generals of the Han Dynasty. The first of them was successful but not able. The second was an able man who happened to fail and is named here to indicate the general about whom the poem is written. Lu Lun's *Border Songs* concern Li Kuang, also Wang Ch'ang-ling's *Over the Border*.

The original reference to the gushing water specifies " in Su-lê " and concerns Kên Kung, a general of the Han Dynasty who, surrounded by the Tartars in Su-lê City, was without water, but who prayed and was answered by the gushing of a spring which saved his men.

In the next line the original text names Ying-chüan, the native place of Kuan Fu, who is thereby indicated and who was a general of the Han Dynasty, a wine-drinking mischief-maker.

In the original the last two lines refer definitely to " the Prefect of Yün-chung." This was Wêi Shang of the Han Dynasty. He was a venerable official at Yüng-chung near the Tartar border and was removed on account of his age. But when the Tartars began to advance, he was restored to his post by the Emperor and gave distinguished service.

112. Nan-king, called formerly and in the original of this poem Chin-ling, was the capital of the Six Dynasties (317–589).

113. In Giles's *History of Chinese Literature* the latter two lines of this poem are mistakenly ascribed to Tu Fu.

114. Sent by the Emperor Wu Ti of Han (140–87 B.C.) as envoy to the Huns, Su Wu was held captive by them near the Gobi Desert and lived there for nineteen years as a shepherd. When he returned, in 86 B.C., the first year of the reign of Chao Ti, he was rewarded with " two paltry millions and the chancellorship of the Tributary States . . . not a foot of soil . . . while some cringing courtier gets the marquisate of ten thousand families." Poems of great beauty and interest were interchanged between Su Wu and the renegade general Li Ling.

115. In the original text of the second line the poet, indicating himself, names Ch'ien-lou, a well-known but indigent scholar who finally starved to death; and in the later lines which we translate

> There have been better men than I to whom heaven
> denied a son,

> There was a poet better than I whose dead wife could
> not hear him,

the original text specifies Têng Yu, a man of good character and conduct, to whom Heaven was deaf and unjust, granting him no sons, and P'an Yüeh, a writer famous for his elegies to his wife.

The unknown Chinese editor entitled this volume " three hundred poems"; the number, as in the Confucian collection, being slightly inexact.

ACKNOWLEDGMENTS

For carefully recording and helpfully shaping Dr. Kiang's dictation of the literal texts of one of the two Chinese volumes comprising this work — the volume containing the longer poems — I am indebted to a well-chosen pupil and friend of his and mine, Mr. Will Garrett. For pertinent and wise suggestions I am grateful to Mr. Arthur Davison Ficke, Mr. Porter Garnett, Mr. Haniel Long, Mrs. Julia Ellsworth Ford, Mr. Cliff McCarthy, Dr. Hu Suh, Mr. Nieh Shih-chang, and Princess Der Ling.

Two hundred and seventy-eight of the poems have been printed in the following magazines and journals:

The Freeman, Asia, The Nation, Poetry, Orient, The International Interpreter, Palms, The New York Evening Post, The New Republic, The Dial, The Bookman, The China Review, The Christian Century, Contemporary Verse, The Double Dealer, The Forum, The Fugitive, The Harvard Advocate, Hearst's, Holland's, The Independent, The Little Review, The Measure, The Lyric, The Midland, The Modern Review, The New Orient, The North-China Herald, The Outlook, Parnassus, Pegasus, Phantasmus, The Review, Rhythmus, Shadowland, The Smart Set, The Poetry Folio, The Southwest Review, Voices, The Wave, The World Tomorrow, The Virginia Quarterly Review, Tambour, Beau, Caprice, The Santa Fe New Mexican, Pearson's Magazine and The London Mercury.

The preface, *Poetry and Culture,* appeared in the Dial, and an expanded form of it under the title, *The Persistence of Poetry* is being privately printed as a book by The Book Club of California.

W. B.

Index of Titles

Index of Titles

Index of First Lines

Index of First Lines

WITTER BYNNER was born in Brooklyn, New York, in 1881. After his graduation from Harvard, Bynner became assistant editor of *McClure's Magazine,* and at the same time literary adviser for McClure, Phillips & Company. After the success of his first book of poems, *Young Harvard* (1907), he lived for a decade in Cornish, New Hampshire, writing and publishing poetry. This was followed by a year of teaching a course in verse-writing at the University of California. After this he traveled extensively in the Orient, particularly in China, and Chinese poetry became a great literary influence in his life. Bynner's translation, with Dr. Kiang Kang-hu, of the poems included in *The Jade Moutain* (1929) made up the first volume of Chinese verse to be translated in full by an American poet. He died in 1968.

VINTAGE CRITICISM,
LITERATURE, MUSIC, AND ART

VINTAGE BIOGRAPHY AND AUTOBIOGRAPHY

V-285   PARKES, HENRY B. *Gods and Men*

V-719   REED, JOHN *Ten Days That Shook the World*

V-176   SCHAPIRO, LEONARD *The Government and Politics of the Soviet Union* (Revised Edition)

V-745   SCHAPIRO, LEONARD *The Communist Party of the Soviet Union*

V-375   SCHURMANN, F. and O. SCHELL (eds.) *The China Reader: Imperial China,* I

V-376   SCHURMANN, F. and O. SCHELL (eds.) *The China Reader: Republican China,* II

V-377   SCHURMANN, F. and O. SCHELL (eds.) *The China Reader: Communist China,* III

V-681   SNOW, EDGAR *Red China Today*

V-312   TANNENBAUM, FRANK *Ten Keys to Latin America*

V-322   THOMPSON, E. P. *The Making of the English Working Class*

V-724   WALLACE, SIR DONALD MACKENZIE *Russia: On the Eve of War and Revolution*

V-206   WALLERSTEIN, IMMANUEL *Africa: The Politics of Independence*

V-298   WATTS, ALAN *The Way of Zen*

V-557   WEINSTEIN, JAMES *The Decline of Socialism in America 1912-1925*

V-106   WINSTON, RICHARD *Charlemagne: From the Hammer to the Cross*

V-627   WOMACK, JOHN JR. *Zapata and the Mexican Revolution*

V-81   WOOCK, ROGER R. and ARTHUR I. BLAUSTEIN (eds.) *Man against Poverty: World War III*

V-486   WOOLF, S. J. (ed.) *European Fascism*

V-545   WOOLF, S. J. (ed.) *The Nature of Fascism*

V-495   YGLESIAS, JOSE *In the Fist of Revolution: Life in a Cuban Country Town*